Using Primary Sources in the Classroom

Examining
Our Past

Understanding
Our Present

Considering
Our Future

Author
Kathleen Vest, M.A. Ed.

SHELL EDUCATION

Contributing Author
Leni Donlan

Editor
Stephanie Macceca, M.A. Ed.

Editorial Project Manager
Emily R. Smith, M.A. Ed.

Editor-in-Chief
Sharon Coan, M.S. Ed.

Art Director
Lee Aucoin

Cover Designer
Lesley Palmer

Cover Art
The Library of Congress
The Burton Family

Imaging
Alfred Lau

Production Manager
Phil Garcia

Publisher
Corinne Burton, M.A. Ed.

Shell Education

5301 Oceanus Drive
Huntington Beach, CA 92649-1030

http://www.shelleducation.com

ISBN 978-1-4258-0367-4

© 2005 Shell Educational Publishing, Inc.

Table of Contents

Introduction

What Are Primary Sources?

Every day, people create and use items that leave clues about their lives and about the workings of governments or businesses. These items include personal papers, letters, notes, oral accounts, diaries, maps, recipes, photographs, reports, novels, poetry, stories (written and spoken), artifacts, coins, stamps, drawings, handiwork, newspapers, books, government documents, business documents, and many others.

Figure 1.1

The contents of Abraham Lincoln's pockets on the night of his assassination, April 14, 1865
Source: The Library of Congress

The Historical Record

Historians call this evidence the historical record. Though it is great in scope, the historical record gives us but a tiny glimpse into the past. Much evidence was never documented or has been lost or destroyed. However, the people who have been interested in history have purposefully left resources such as journals, diaries, autobiographies, recorded family trees, personal letters, and business papers. Historians use all possible resources available, which include both primary and secondary sources, to answer questions about the past.

Figure 1.2

The Daily Citizen—*Vicksburg, Mississippi, Thursday, July 2, 1863*
Source: The Library of Congress

What Is a Primary Source?

Primary sources are part of direct personal experiences of a time or event. They are original items or records that have survived from the past, such as clothing, letters, photographs, and manuscripts. The photograph above (Figure 1.1) shows a primary source from the night of President Abraham Lincoln's assassination in 1865.

What Is a Secondary Source?

Secondary sources may have been created immediately after or long after an event took place. These sources document or analyze someone else's experience. They provide a perspective or a description of past events. The resources students use in a typical school environment, such as history textbooks or encyclopedias, are secondary sources written long after the historical events they describe took place. The newspaper to the left (Figure 1.2) is an example of a secondary source from the Civil War Era.

Types of Primary Sources

Figure 1.3a

Silver-plated spurs
Source: The Library of Congress

Figure 1.3b

Old chisel
Source: The Library of Congress

Artifacts

Artifacts are physical objects that have survived from the recent or distant past. They include tools, weapons, inventions, coins and paper money (which is also a document), clothing, uniforms, political campaign items, pottery, and cooking utensils. Because they provide a solid, tactile connection to the past, artifacts can help immerse students in history. The silver-plated spurs and old chisel (Figures 1.3a and 1.3b) are examples of artifacts from the old West.

Artifacts offer a glimpse into the lives of those who created them and an opportunity to consider the technology, tools, and materials available through time. Artifacts provide concrete evidence of advances in technology and of the changes that occur over time. They stimulate great curiosity and healthy speculation as students try to understand what they are and how they were used.

Documents

The public can easily access published documents and public record documents. Published documents are created for large audiences and are intended for wide distribution. Published documents include books, magazines, newspapers, reports, laws, advertisements, maps, pamphlets, posters, manuscripts, paper money, and stamps. They are created to keep track of and archive information about citizens, businesses, and government processes. They include press releases, government documents, laws, constitutions, congressional activities, presidential speeches, deeds, land surveys, census data, court records, and voter registration lists. It is important for students to understand that not everything that was published is accurate or reliable. However, even biased sources share important information about the past.

This poster (Figure 1.4) encouraged the purchase of war stamps and bonds to support the war effort during World War II. As illustrated here, published documents might have been produced for public persuasion. Some published documents, in sharing the language or sentiments of another time, may be considered offensive by today's standards. Sensitive treatment of such materials can allow educators to utilize history "in the raw."

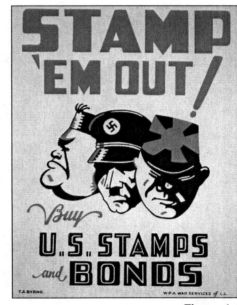

Figure 1.4

Stamp 'em out: Buy U.S. Stamps and Bonds
Source: The Library of Congress

Types of Primary Sources *(cont.)*

Documents *(cont.)*

Unpublished documents and personal papers are seldom meant to be read by the public or to be widely distributed. They include personal letters and diaries, journals, agendas, telegrams, e-mails, wills, correspondence, financial ledgers, meeting minutes, speeches, architectural drawings, blueprints, data listed in family Bibles, research files, tax returns, and classified documents. They offer an intimate glimpse into the lives of individuals or community groups from long ago. These documents not only immerse students in the past, but also provide opportunities to compare and contrast the past to life today. An example of this is an unpublished letter (Figure 1.5) written by President Theodore Roosevelt to his son in 1890.

Oral Histories and Interviews

Long before written accounts of history were created, information was passed from one generation to the next through the spoken word. The cultural or historical information passed by word-of-mouth is called oral history. Oral history includes songs, narratives, and accounts of ethnic traditions. Oral traditions are particularly important for learning the history of minority groups, who were often excluded from mainstream publications or did not leave written sources.

Historians collect oral histories to share, as authentically as possible, with future generations. Participating in projects that require collecting oral histories provides students with a unique opportunity to engage in "making" history. Interviews and recordings of community elders and witnesses to historical events uncover exciting stories, anecdotes, and information about the past. Learning about the past from those who "lived" it breathes life into history. It humanizes events and people that might otherwise be just dry facts and names in a textbook. It helps students understand that history is about people— people like themselves. Figures 1.6a and 1.6b show two different types of oral histories being collected.

Figure 1.5

Letter from Theodore Roosevelt to his son, July 11, 1890
Source: The Library of Congress

Figure 1.6a

Charley Williams tells stories to his granddaughter
Source: The Library of Congress

Figure 1.6b

Fieldworker David Taylor interviews Anne Murphy in 1918
Source: The Library of Congress

Types of Primary Sources (cont.)

Paintings, Photographs, and Prints

Images are simply visual documents that record history. Pictures capture a brief moment in time and can be "worth a thousand words." Pictures should not be taken at face value, however. Photographers arrange, compose, and present pictures to tell a story or to make a particular point.

Paintings and prints are composed by an artist and can have realistic or abstract components. Paintings and prints depicting famous people and historic events are usually those considered in social studies classrooms and these paintings are often romanticized to please the subject or to dramatically portray an event.

Learning to "read" images can provide students with another means of understanding events, objects, and people. Analyzing images can be quite engaging and provides an excellent entry point to complex, inquiry-based learning.

To analyze images well, students need to be taught to carefully observe, activate prior knowledge, draw reasonable conclusions, and determine what further information is needed to more completely understand the visual evidence.

Examine Figures 1.7a and 1.7b. What details do you see? What do you think you know about these people? What do you want to find out? Simple questions like these can lead to more in-depth inquiries.

Figure 1.7a

Baptism near Mineola, Texas
Source: The Library of Congress

The image above (Figure 1.7a) is from 1935. It shows a group of men baptizing a young man in a Texas river. Students can use this photograph as a starting point in researching about different religious practices.

This picture (Figure 1.7b) features a family of eastern European immigrants. Many immigrants who had adequate money had portrait-style photographs taken as they arrived in America. The styles of the clothing and the facial expressions are the main emphasis for student analysis.

Figure 1.7b

Eastern European immigrant family
Source: Courtesy of the Coan family

Types of Primary Sources *(cont.)*

Maps

Even though maps are classified as documents, in this book they will have their own category. Maps require specialized teaching strategies because they contain specific graphics and details. Antique maps (like Figure 1.8) are particularly fascinating to study— they show what people hundreds of years ago imagined the world to be. Large areas that we now inhabit are missing from these maps, yet we have to admire how well our ancestors drew images of their known world with only crude instruments to calculate their measurements.

Figure 1.8

John Smith's map of Virginia
Source: Historical Documents Co.

Cartoons

Political cartoons are satires or graphic commentaries about government decisions, public figures, and current events. To understand their meanings, viewers must have special information. They must understand certain symbols used by cartoonists, they must have knowledge about the current events depicted in the cartoon, and they must be able to analyze the cartoon in order to get the idea that is being portrayed. This is a tall order for students. The National Archives suggests using political cartoons only at the ends of your units of study. That way, students have sufficient knowledge to correctly interpret the work.

Entertainment cartoons, such as *Peanuts, Garfield, Dennis the Menace*, and *Family Circle*, are easier to understand and are a good beginning step for students to grasp the concepts of cartooning. These cartoons also pull from current ideas and social customs, which require students to use both their senses of humor and their analytical skills to understand the underlying meanings of the cartoons.

Examine the "Shocked at Corruption" cartoon (Figure 1.9). What are the symbols in the cartoon? What do they mean? What is the theme of the cartoon? Questions like these are beginning of an in-depth study.

Figure 1.9

Harper's Weekly—*Shocked at Corruption*
Source: The Library of Congress

Types of Primary Sources *(cont.)*

Sound Recordings and Films

Sound or audio recordings include interviews, music, popular songs, famous political speeches, and broadcasts from radio and television. Examples of recording materials include band music from the Civil War Era (such as Figure 1.10), regional ethnic and folk culture music, presidential inaugural speeches, and entertainment from the days of vaudeville to the early days of radio and motion pictures.

Sounds tell us a great deal about an era. For example, how does the language and content of an old radio broadcast differ from what we see or hear on radio and television today? What can we learn from song lyrics about historical events of another era or about the beliefs and cultural values of that time?

Films visually capture moments in time and can provide indicators of changes over time. Evidence about a culture at specific moments in history can be uniquely conveyed in film. Through visual and audio clues, filmmakers reveal the customs, preferences, styles, special occasions, occupations, and recreational activities that existed during a specific historical period.

While films may create a compelling sense of authenticity, students must realize that, like other primary sources, a film has a creator with a point of view. Students should consider: What was the creator's purpose in making this film? Why was a specific setting used? Why was a certain perspective shown? How did the filmmaker choose the framing and distance used? Why was this subject chosen? What was included, and what was excluded?

Figure 1.10

The Black Brigade: Plantation Song and Dance
Source: The Library Congress

A Word about Primary Source Categories

Categories are not always easy to define when working with primary sources. For example, paper money can be considered an artifact or a published document. Posters can be considered documents or prints. Some advertising posters resemble cartoons. Discussions about what primary sources fit where can be entertaining for students and adults with inquiring natures. However, this type of technical discussion is not necessary for every grade level.

The introduction and exploration of documents are activities teachers can enjoy with their students. Numerous strategies are available in this book that can make the primary source adventure easier and more fascinating for the classroom.

Why Use Primary Sources in the Classroom?

Primary sources add a real-life element to history. With primary sources, history changes from a textbook study of events to a more intimate focus on the humans who participated in that history. When students read a soldier's letter, analyze parts of a famous document, study a picture of child laborers, interpret an old map, read an oral history of a woman who marched in a suffrage parade, or touch an old artifact, they walk in the shoes of their forefathers for a moment in time. History becomes a series of stories about real people who had families, jobs, and dreams. Students begin to realize that the people throughout history had goals to accomplish and difficulties to endure. Students also begin to understand their own ties to the past. They will learn that other generations not only had many differences from people today, but also had many similarities. Ultimately, students can discover how to research both primary and secondary sources to answer their questions and form educated conclusions.

This section discusses how primary sources help students:

- develop observation skills.

- develop vocabulary and reading-comprehension skills.

- develop inquiry skills.

- understand that history has local links.

- develop empathy for the human condition.

- analyze different points of view.

- understand that history is a continuum and that people all make their own personal histories.

- prepare for state and national tests that use document-based questions.

- develop research skills that lead to analyzing sources and forming conclusions.

When taking students through the primary-source adventure, there are several steps to consider. First, students learn how to make observations about a variety of primary sources. They gain reading and vocabulary skills for encountering the sophisticated text contained in many documents. Students will also learn how to write appropriate questions about what they have observed or read and find possible answers. Depending on the type of source they are viewing, students consider what local links the source contains; how to empathize with the human condition the source reveals; what points of view the source demonstrates; and how the source fits into the continuum of history. Judging the source in its historical context is also an important step for older students. Obviously, elementary students and high school students can investigate primary sources on different levels. Teachers are the best judges for what their students can do with different sources. Further steps for working with primary sources involve assessing students' responses to the source when they use graphic organizers, write responses, draw researched conclusions, or create projects. These ideas will be explored further in each chapter.

Why Use Primary Sources in the Classroom? *(cont.)*

Primary sources help students develop observation skills . . .

Viewing document facsimiles, photographs, prints, artifacts, maps, and political cartoons requires students to observe details and make assumptions. What type of primary source is this? Who made it? Why was it made? What are the most important things about this primary source? Does it contain symbols or images? Are there any clues about how life was different in the time this primary source was made?

The seal of Plymouth (Figure 1.11), has four different, yet similar, images. Students can also try to read the meanings of the Latin words. They might enjoy using a magnifying glass or hand lens to analyze details.

Figure 1.11
First Seal of Plymouth

Primary sources help students develop vocabulary and reading-comprehension skills . . .

With teacher-guided instruction, elementary and middle school students can learn to read excerpts from documents, and high school students can tackle whole documents. Through the use of vocabulary activities, such as constructing a document word chart, students will become familiar with legal jargon, archaic phrases, and formal language. In this book, specific strategies will be described in the published documents and unpublished documents chapters.

Primary sources help students develop inquiry skills . . .

Students spend much of their time responding to teacher or state-generated questions. However, learning to ask questions and then research answers are also essential ingredients to effective learning. Inquiring minds are needed in a democratic form of government. By their very nature, primary sources call for an inquiry approach and sometimes raise more questions than they answer.

Why Use Primary Sources in the Classroom? *(cont.)*

Primary sources help students develop inquiry skills *(cont.)*

Figure 1.12 is a photo of child laborers by Lewis W. Hine. Its original caption reads: "Bibb Mill No. 1 Macon, Georgia. Many youngsters here. Some boys and girls were so small they had to climb up on the spinning frame to mend the broken threads and to put back the empty bobbins. Photo dated 1/19/1909." Studying this photo automatically causes students to ask questions and compare their own lives to the children in the photo. On the Internet, there are many more child-labor photos that can be used as a collection for studying this topic. Students can then research the development of the Child Labor Law that now protects children . . . and maybe students will realize how fortunate they are today.

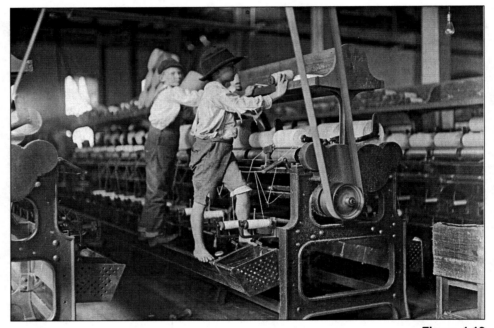

Figure 1.12

Child laborers in Macon, Georgia
Source: The National Archives, Lewis W. Hine Collection

Primary sources stand as pieces of evidence generated by people in the past. For that reason, they are open for interpretation. Working with primary sources gives students the engaging opportunity to become "history detectives." As students search the elements of a primary source for hidden clues, they begin to develop questions. How was this machine used? Why did these people think this way? What event was taking place and why were the people there? Why did these people pose for this picture? Questions like these engage learners and lead to a quest for answers. As a result, teachers can demonstrate to students the effective tools for researching to find answers—or to discover even more questions. Students soon learn that true research is sometimes a maze of facts and opinions, and that sorting through these clues is what a history detective does in order to learn. Students can be junior historians rather than just test takers as a direct result of working with primary sources.

Why Use Primary Sources in the Classroom? *(cont.)*

Primary sources help students understand that history has local links . . .

Most textbooks focus on major world events, national events, and famous people. Little is written about the vast majority of citizens whose daily lives affect and are affected by such events and trends. Each family and every community has its own history. And, some of that history is tied directly to national and world events. When family members go to war, they become part of a major world event, and their family feels the impact of the war more keenly. The communications between soldiers and their families are primary sources that give insight into world events from personal points of view. In addition, a community's history may be tied to certain immigration trends. Family stories and artifacts pertaining to the immigration process are intimate reflections of a larger world or national picture.

Exposing students to local historical research increases their understanding of the people and places they already know. Figures 1.13a and 1.13b show how changes in a local community might be reflected in photographs. Students who conduct oral history interviews of Korean War veterans in their own communities learn how those senior citizens acted and thought as young men facing possible death. Visiting local antique shops to find kitchen artifacts from the turn of the century gives students opportunities to understand how much more time consuming household chores were in the past.

Teachers can develop projects that help students share their own stories—stories about familiar people, places, and events. Exploring the primary sources in their own homes can help students recognize that family history is linked to national and world history. Sometimes starting with questions that students ask family members can provide interesting stories to share with class members. Questions for students to ask someone over the age of 50 would be: *"Where were you when President Kennedy was assassinated, and what was your reaction to that event?"* and *"What are your best and worst memories about elementary, junior high, or senior high?"*

However, a word of caution is in order when focusing on family history projects in which students research family trees. Some students may have had a major change in their family structure, and family research projects may be considered too personal by some parents or guardians. Please be mindful of the pain involved for some when researching their own histories, and try to be flexible with reluctant students and parents.

Figure 1.13a

Virginia intersection in 1935
Source: Courtesy of Kathryn Kiley

Figure 1.13b

Virginia intersection today
Source: Courtesy of Emily R. Smith

Why Use Primary Sources in the Classroom? *(cont.)*

Primary sources help students develop empathy for the human condition . . .

Adults and students seldom choose to curl up and read a textbook, yet many enjoy reading historical fiction. Historical fiction has well-developed characters, action, and insights into how the historical figures were feeling and thinking. Reading *The Witch of Blackbird Pond* or *The Crucible* can give the reader more empathy for the people experiencing the horrors of witch trials in their community than reading a textbook account of the trials. Historical fiction writers focus on the human condition. They humanize their characters with emotions and motivations that remind students of their own experiences and feelings. The characters emulate real people with real problems.

It is one thing to review a set of statistics about casualties in the Civil War. It is a far different experience to consider the injuries of Civil War soldiers through the letters of Walt Whitman, who visited soldiers in Civil War hospitals.

Primary sources help students relate to events of the past in a personal way. In this notebook entry (Figure 1.14), Whitman recorded notes from his visit with a young soldier named Dolliver. What can we learn about this young soldier from this notebook entry? What will today's students think and feel when they realize just how young this soldier was? To what events in the world today might this young soldier's situation be compared?

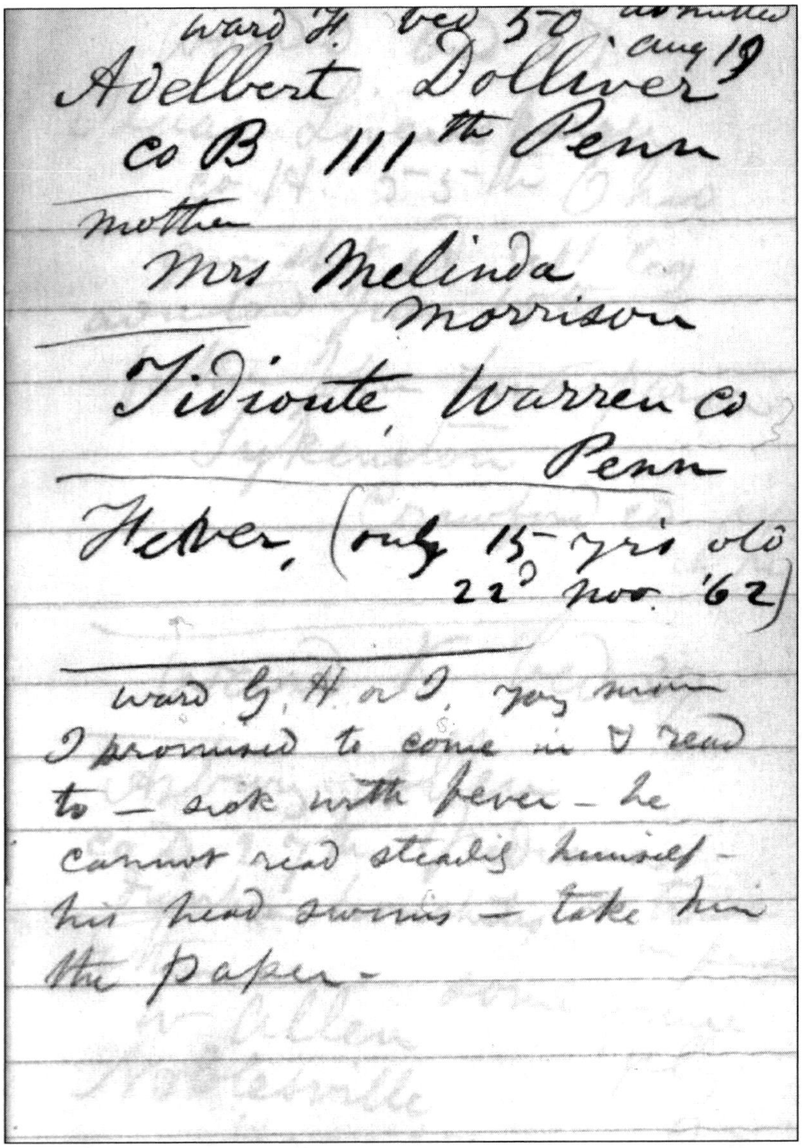

ward H. bed 50 admitted Aug 19
Adelbert Dolliver
Co B 111th Penn
mother
Mrs Melinda Morrison
Tidioute, Warren Co Penn
Fever, (only 15 yrs old
22d Nov. '62)
ward G, H or I, young man
I promised to come in & read
to — sick with fever — he
cannot read steadily himself —
his head swims — take him
the paper —

Figure 1.14
Walt Whitman's hospital notebook
Source: The Library of Congress

Why Use Primary Sources in the Classroom? *(cont.)*

Primary sources help students analyze different points of view . . .

We know that two people viewing the same painting or photograph may see it very differently, just as two people can hear something differently in the same conversation or musical selection. People who witness the same event can even report seeing very different things. Jurors observing the same case frequently remember different aspects of the trial and focus on different testimonies. Why? These different viewpoints happen because people carry around "perceptual baggage." This baggage consists of expectations, biases, values, and prior experiences that often affect what they see or hear. This is a human condition that our legal system recognizes and has tried to address through a twelve-juror panel.

In analyzing primary sources, students learn to both understand inferences and to make their own inferences. One critical inference is point of view. Students should understand that the speaker, the photographer, the musician, or the cartographer who created a speech, photograph, song, or map had a reason for creating it and a point to emphasize. Students need to consider the point of view of the creator of the artifact, both from the personal aspect and from the era in which that person lived. A man living in 1875 had a different point of view about women's suffrage than a man living today has due to his own cultural heritage.

Figure 1.15 shows a pile of 40,000 bison hides in 1878. Students viewing this photo can examine different points of view about hunting animals in the nineteenth century West. They can then discuss why people in the twenty-first century are so critical of this kind of hunting and why many people in the mid-nineteenth century were unconcerned.

Analyzing viewpoints within historical contexts helps students understand that *judging* the past is a more in-depth process than just making quick criticisms through modern eyes. While it is important to understand the mistakes of the past, it can also be revealing to realize that many times people in the past just did the best they could with the information that they had at their time. It can also be an eye-opening experience to learn that some day other generations may also judge us and criticize our archaic practices and viewpoints.

Figure 1.15

*Bison hide yard in 1878,
Dodge City, Kansas*
Source: The National Archives

Why Use Primary Sources in the Classroom? *(cont.)*

Primary sources help students understand that history is a continuum and that people all make their own personal histories . . .

We all participate in making history every day. In the course of our lives, each of us leaves behind primary source documentation that future scholars may examine as a record of "the past." We create many records of our activities (diaries, personal notes, letters to friends or relatives, e-mail messages, or telephone messages), while traces of our activities appear in records created by others
(a friend's diary, notes, or calendar entry; a letter or e-mail from a friend or relative). Further traces of our activities occur in school records (registration records, report cards, awards, disciplinary action), in business records (checks, charge card receipts, sales receipts), in school or local newspapers, in government records (driver's licenses, registrations, tax records). In addition, people can offer testimony (oral history) about their activities.

When students understand that everyone makes history every day, their capacity to truly understand history is immensely increased.

Figure 1.16 is the first page of a letter that Harry S. Truman wrote to his girlfriend, Bess Wallace. He is apologizing for getting ill and not being able to take her to a performance. The letter gives us a view of courting practices from another era and how Truman, a man who would later lead the free world, was once a shy, young man seeking a young woman's approval. The other seven pages of the letter are included on the CD-ROM for your reference. (See pages 173–176 for more information.)

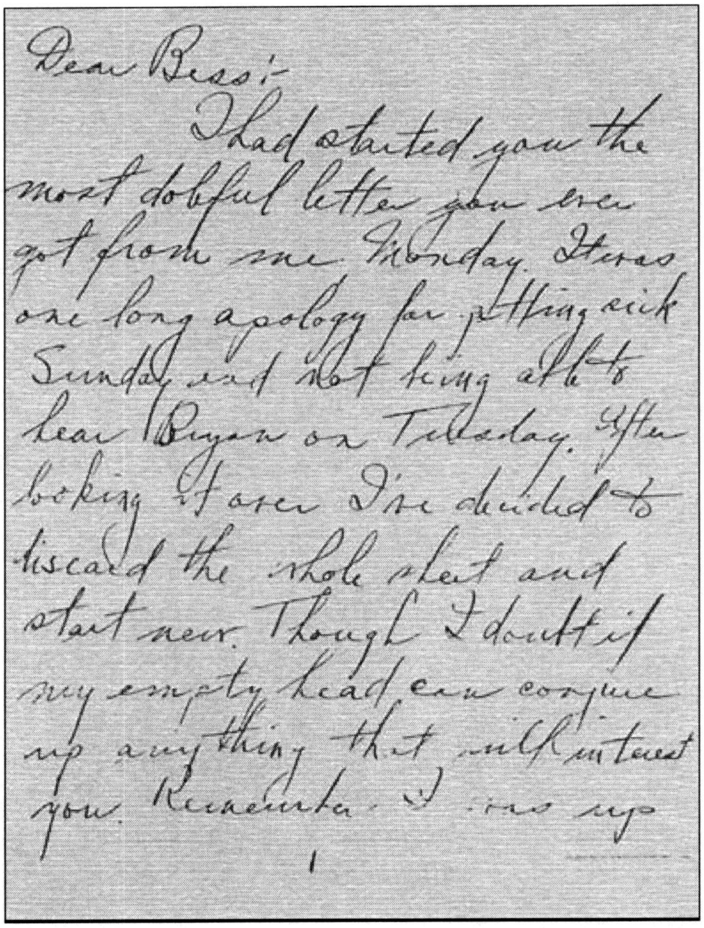

Dear Bess:-

I had started you the most dobful letter you ever got from me Monday. It was one long apology for getting sick Sunday and not being able to hear Bryan on Tuesday. After looking it over I've decided to discard the whole sheet and start new. Though I doubt if my empty head can conjure up anything that will interest you. Remember I was up

Figure 1.16

Harry S. Truman letter to Bess Wallace, July 17, 1911

Source: Truman Presidential Museum and Library

Why Use Primary Sources in the Classroom? *(cont.)*

Primary sources help students prepare for state and national tests that use document-based questions . . .

The reality of the teaching world today is that tests rule much of what must be taught. More and more, tests are focused on having students construct responses rather than select the correct answer from a list. State and national tests require students to analyze graphs, charts, lists, documents, maps, photos, political cartoons, and pictures of artifacts. When students use primary sources in the classroom on a regular basis, they are better equipped to deal with test items requiring analytical thinking and responses.

On pages 163–168 of this book is a section that explains how to develop document-based assessments. The section also provides scoring guidelines to help evaluate student work. Teachers within any state testing program or advanced placement (AP) program that uses document-based questions will find that primary sources should be an integral part of their classrooms.

Primary sources help students develop research skills that lead to analyzing sources and forming opinions . . .

The ultimate goal of exposing students to primary sources in the classroom is that they will learn to research and select primary sources to support themes, questions, research papers, and projects that they develop. From primary sources, students can gather data, opinions, ideas, and facts. They can then sift through all this information to form their own conclusions. Learning to use primary sources as supportive evidence in research projects will enable students to produce a high-quality and more-accurate presentation.

Technology-based research projects will probably be quite appealing to your students. They will want to find primary sources online, research online, and then transfer what they have gathered and learned into multimedia projects, Web quests, or Web pages. These are all excellent projects. However, students using online resources may end up cutting and pasting rather than researching, reading, analyzing, and summarizing. Thus, students need direct instruction in taking what they have read or viewed and developing their own interpretations and conclusions.

Why Use Primary Sources in the Classroom? *(cont.)*

Technology Projects and Copyright Issues

Students designing multimedia presentations for the classroom may copy photo images and documents from the Internet without any copyright infringement . . . as long as they cite their sources correctly. However, it is critical that students understand that making Web pages that are available online is considered publishing, and they need permission to use most photo images or documents on their created websites. Students can supply links to photos on other websites without obtaining copyright permission, but they cannot copy photographs to their sites. Do not assume that materials on government websites, such as the Library of Congress and the National Archives, are in the public domain. Many of these documents are in the public domain, but others are online by permission from those who hold the copyrights. Students designing Web quests can set up a list of links, but they cannot transfer published documents to their quests' Web pages without permission. Time spent reviewing these rules with your students is essential in this era of Internet-based research and showcasing.

The images used throughout this book are all included on the Teacher Resource CD. On pages 173–176 is a detailed listing of where the original images are located along with filenames of the images.

National History Day

One significant avenue for primary source research is to engage students in the National History Day project. National History Day is a contest where students create a history-focused exhibit, documentary, paper, or performance based on a yearly theme. The project must feature student research using primary and secondary resources. Students have the opportunity to win awards and scholarships.

There are two divisions in National History Day competitions: Junior (grades 6–8) and Senior (grades 9–12). Students may participate as individuals or as part of a group of up to five students. Students participate in a local contest. The local winners then go to state contests, and those winners participate in the national contest held in the summer at the University of Maryland. Visit the National History Day website (http://www.nationalhistoryday.org/) to get ideas for this year's theme and the rules and regulations. Some presidential libraries or other museums support the local contests, so contacting their education departments can give teachers a chance to get great advice.

Paintings, Photographs, and Prints

Overview

The old cliché that "a picture is worth a thousand words" certainly applies to using prints, photographs, paintings, illustrations, and engravings as primary sources in the classroom. Students are drawn to pictures and the stories they reveal. Certain historical pictures stay in the public mind. Little John Kennedy saluting his father's casket as it passed by is a photograph that captures the emotions of a nation. Old photographs remind us of where we have been.

This photograph of Flagstaff, Arizona, (Figure 2.1) in the late 1800s is a reminder of a very different lifestyle—one totally foreign to residents of that city today.

Figure 2.1

Flagstaff, Arizona
Source: The National Archives

Below (Figure 2.2) is the portrait of a proud immigrant couple dressed in their finest clothing. This links us to people who left one world behind them to discover a new world of opportunity.

Prints, drawings, photographs, paintings, and illustrations are some of the first primary sources that young children study. Children have early experiences with picture books that require them to respond to different pages full of images. Parents and teachers ask children questions about what they see. How many fish are in this picture? Why is that little boy crying? Therefore, it naturally follows that even young children can study and appreciate primary source images. In a similar, yet more sophisticated fashion, middle school through university students can also be engaged in examining "picture" primary sources.

This chapter discusses teaching strategies for using photos, paintings, and prints in the classroom. The chapter lists some generic ideas, provides more detailed examples and strategies as the chapter progresses, and ends with three model lessons. The chapter divides the picture primary sources into subsets. Paintings are divided into two categories: general paintings and painted portraits. Photographs are also divided into categories: strong focal-point photographs; photographs with multiple elements; landscapes and waterscapes; photographs of architectural structures; photographic portraits; and photographs of artifacts. The chapter also discusses prints.

Figure 2.2

Mediterranean immigrants
Source: The Burton Family

Locating Paintings, Photographs, and Prints

Family, school, and newspaper photos are quick and easy choices to use in the classroom. Students can analyze the different parts of photos and draw conclusions. Students can study prints and paintings in art books and in other secondary sources. To use a variety of historical photographs, paintings, and prints, teachers need to gain access to collections in museums, county or state archives, national institutions, and presidential libraries. Online resources at the National Archives, the Library of Congress, numerous historic museums, state archives, and presidential libraries offer so many options that a teacher's most difficult task will be wading through all the possibilities to make selections. (See pages 171–172 for further information about online options.)

Getting Started

Exposing students to historical photos and prints at an early age and on a regular basis prepares them to handle these items appropriately on future tests and to understand how to examine clues from the past. Primary sources become interesting and even fun to use and examine. They are not just something confusing to study a few weeks before an exam. To begin the process of studying primary source images, use examples from the everyday lives of students:

1. Ask younger children to bring in a few photos to share and post. Explain to them that the photos they brought are primary sources and that some day their children and grandchildren will be interested in how the people in those pictures lived, dressed, and acted. Share some photos you have brought from your childhood, and let the students discuss ways your photos may be different from theirs. Have students imagine what their grandchildren might ask about these photos.

2. Hold up examples of students' artwork and share with them that they have created primary sources—original works that could become part of an archive collection. As students peruse portfolios of their own work, explain that they are really viewing a collection of original work that would be of interest to them or their families in the future.

3. Share a book of artistic prints with the class and let students discuss the pictures. Tell the class that they are looking at primary source prints that were reproduced (copied) and made into books for sale. The artists made original sketches and/or prints, which are the original primary sources, just as the students' pictures are original.

4. Choose a vivid historic picture to share with your students, and let them discuss what they see in the photograph. For example, ask them how the picture of the American Indian family (Figure 2.3) on the following page is similar to their family and how it is different from their family. Ask them why they think the photograph was taken.

Locating Paintings, Photographs, and Prints *(cont.)*

General Questions and Activities

In these pages, many strategies for using photographs, prints, or paintings will be described, illustrated, and detailed. However, to begin teaching with primary sources, select from this set of generic prompts. Choose the prompts that suit the images and ages of your students.

- What type of picture is this? (photograph, painting, print, portrait, engraving)

- What is the style of the picture? (landscape, group picture, historical scene, portrait, graphic design, still life)

- Describe the people or objects in the picture.

- Describe the setting.

- Describe the activity (action) in the picture.

- What things in this picture are familiar to you—things you already know about?

- What things in this picture are unfamiliar to you—things you do not know about or understand?

- What questions do you have about this picture?

- How could you find the answers to your questions?

- What are two inferences you could make about this picture?

- Why was this photograph taken, picture painted, or print designed?

- What is the point of view of the photographer or artist?

- Why is this image historically important?

Figure 2.3
American Indian family
Source: Denver Public Library, Charles Nast

Locating Paintings, Photographs, and Prints *(cont.)*

General Questions and Activities *(cont.)*

Here are some general activities to use when students study photographs, prints, or paintings. Choose the activities that fit the images and ages of your students.

- **Divided Image**

  This is an activity that will be suggested often in this book. First, divide the picture into four sections or two parts to make it easier to examine. Then, have students list everything they see in their assigned sections of the picture.

- **Column List**

  Make a three-column list of the people, objects, and activities in the picture.

- **Point of View**

  Write about the picture from the point of view of one of the people or objects in the picture.

- **Caption Writing**

  Write a detailed caption for the picture.

- **Prequel/Sequel Writing**

  Write what you think happened before or after the picture.

- **Dialogue**

  Write a conversation between two people or objects in the picture.

- **News Writing**

  Write a newspaper story about the picture.

- **Compare and Contrast**

  Design a two-column chart for students to compare or contrast elements in the picture or to compare or contrast two whole pictures.

Paintings

Paintings as primary sources are viewed in a gallery or as facsimiles in the classroom. They are original creations that strongly focus on the creator's point of view, his or her talent, and the era in which the painting was created. A painting can be landscape, waterscape, portrait, still life, action, or graphic in design and can be analyzed artistically or historically.

In this book, the focus is the historical aspects of the subject matter within the painting rather than the artistic. If the painting is about a historic event, the artist frequently has portrayed the event in a stylized or glorified manner. The artist may have assembled elements from the event to tell a story or to make a point, rather than try to accurately depict an exact moment in history.

Discussion Questions: The following questions can be used in junction with most historical paintings. The questions range in complexity.

- What was the artist's purpose in painting this image?
- What event is taking place? Does it appear to be a real or staged event? What action is happening?
- Who is the artist? Is he or she famous?
- Who are the main figures in the painting? How are they dressed? What are they doing?
- What is the setting? How does the setting help tell the story in the painting? What objects do you see?
- What is the focal point of the painting?
- How did the artist use light, shadow, color, and lines to get your attention?

In this painting (Figure 2.4), five patriots are assembled to read a draft of the Declaration of Independence. The artist's goal was to show who was involved in forming the ideas in this document, not to correctly portray the actual event. In studying a painting with several characters, students could discuss who the people are, what the setting might be, how people are dressed, what the focal point is, and, in this case, who seems to be in charge of this meeting. Students should also formulate their own questions. Who is the center of attention in this painting, and why? Why were they wearing heavy coats in the summer?

Figure 2.4

Drafting of the Declaration of Independence
Source: The National Archives

Paintings *(cont.)*

Divided Image: In the painting below (Figure 2.5), the artist has depicted Columbus visiting King Ferdinand and Queen Isabella to report about his discoveries on his first voyage. In this case, dividing the picture into two sides can be helpful. Students can list the people on the right side, not by name, but by their roles—priests, sailors, officers, soldiers, Indians, and Columbus. Then, they can list the people and objects on the left side in the same manner. Students can discuss what they think is happening in the painting and why Columbus needed to report to this king and queen. Students can then write three questions that they think the king and queen might have asked Columbus during this meeting.

Figure 2.5

Columbus visiting King Ferdinand and Queen Isabella
Source: The Library of Congress

Dialogue: One activity that students enjoy is writing captions for historic scenes. Show students a set of comic strips with caption bubbles. Explain that within a cartoon strip the meaning of an event is portrayed in the dialogue of the characters, and that they will create dialogue bubbles for real people in a famous painting. Read or explain some of the background of the famous event portrayed in the painting. Photocopy the painting for pairs of students to use. Students may need to do some additional research. Have each pair cut out enough white caption bubbles for the people in the painting. Students then write appropriate comments on the bubbles that they think the main characters in the painting might make during this historic event. Finally, students paste the completed caption bubbles over the head of each person on the photocopied painting.

Note: To give you some practice as you go through this book, you will find assignments that you may choose to either complete on paper, discuss with another teacher, or just think about silently.

Assignment: Choose two questions from the list on page 24 to ask your students for each of the two historical paintings (Figures 2.4 and 2.5). Then, write dialogue for one of the two paintings used in this section.

Painted Portraits

Painted portraits of famous people are popular primary sources. They are interesting on two levels—the person who is the subject of the picture and the artist who painted it. Some portrait painters, like Thomas Gainsborough, became famous, and their styles became quite recognizable.

Discussion Questions: Choose from these questions for studying painted portraits.

- Why was this portrait made?
- What does the clothing tell you about this person?
- What, if anything, is the person holding?
- What is the subject(s) expression?
- What is the background of the portrait?
- Some portraits have symbols or panels telling about the person's life. What do you notice about these panels or symbols? What do you think they mean?

Compare and Contrast: This portrait (Figure 2.6) is a typical three-quarters portrait of a famous man, Supreme Court Justice John Jay in his judge's robes. Comparing portraits with similar themes can be an important historical research task. Students can use a Venn diagram or T-chart in order to compare this portrait to a portrait of a modern-day Supreme Court justice. Teachers can also use this activity with sets of portraits—two presidents, two American Indians, and so on.

Analyzing Art: Figure 2.7 depicts William the Conqueror. It has a portrait in the center and graphic details to portray his accomplishments around the outside. There are many antique portraits of explorers, military leaders, and nobility that use this style of embellished symbolic paneling. Students can examine the actual portrait of William the Conqueror and what he is wearing and holding. They will also need to examine the symbols at the top, the characters on the side, and the miniature scene at the bottom. Using a magnifying glass or hand lens can help students view details. Students can discuss what they think is happening in the bottom scene and side panels, and then make a list of questions they want answered. Encourage them to follow up with research to find the answers.

Assignment: Find two Internet locations that have information on William the Conqueror that might help your students find some answers about the side panels regarding his life and accomplishments.

Figure 2.6

John Jay
Source: The Library of Congress

Figure 2.7

William the Conqueror
Source: The Library of Congress

Photographs

Photographs are familiar types of primary sources. People deal with these sources on a regular basis and may have hundreds of them stashed in a variety of boxes waiting to be sorted. Photographs, unlike paintings, capture the moment in time as it was. However, the photographer may still have had a point of view and certainly may have chosen to capture one image or angle over another at that time. Today, people need to be on guard that photos have not been digitally altered or distorted. Tabloids use various techniques to falsify and exaggerate events, and students need to be on the lookout for such simulated images.

The teaching strategies for photographs have been divided into categories based on the composition of photographs, rather than by the subject matter. The categories are: landscapes and waterscapes, strong focal-point photographs, photographs with multiple elements, photographs of architectural structures, photographic portraits, and photographs of artifacts. In some cases, a photograph falls into two categories such as landscape and strong focal point. In such cases, questions or activities might be selected from both sections to enable students to study the picture in greater depth.

Figure 2.8a
Angel Island
Source: Library of Congress

This **landscape** example has buildings that are part of the whole image composition but are not of particular architectural importance.

Figure 2.8b
Roundup at the ranch
Source: The National Archives

This **strong focal-point** example is a lone cowboy surveying a distant herd.

Figure 2.8c
Building the Berlin Wall
Source: Courtesy of Betsy Morris

This photograph presents **multiple elements** with workers, buildings, fencing, and mounds of earth.

Figure 2.8d
Florence Duomo
Source: Courtesy of Rachelle Cracchiolo

This is a photograph of a building with dramatic **architectural structures** to study.

Figure 2.8e
General Robert E. Lee
Source: The National Archives

This is a **photographic portrait** of General Robert E. Lee by Mathew Brady.

Assignment: Choose the best question from page 26 to ask regarding each photo.

Landscape or Waterscape Photographs

Landscape photographs may have some people, animals, or buildings, but these are not the significant features. The main features are the landforms, natural scenery, and weather conditions. Waterscapes (or seascapes) may have some people, animals, and ships. However, the main feature is the sea, river, bay, canal, and supporting landforms. Antique postcards that feature landscape or waterscape scenes are interesting and inexpensive items for students to study. Students can compare a turn-of-the-century postcard of a park or coastal area to a recent postcard of the same area.

Discussion Questions: Some basic questions for landscape or waterscape photographs are:

- Where do you think this scene is located?
- What are the major elements of this photograph?
- Why is this location important?
- How would you feel if you were in this scene?

Divided Image: Studying the composition of a landscape or waterscape photograph may require visually dividing the space into quadrants; dividing it into halves either horizontally or vertically; or dividing the study into foreground and background. The image to the right (Figure 2.9) of the dust storm in Kansas shows a devastating historic event. Dividing the dust storm photograph in half horizontally makes the students see how huge and thick the dust cloud is in comparison to the size of the homes it will be hitting.

Figure 2.9
Dust storm in Kansas
Source: The National Archives, Franklin D. Roosevelt Library

Column Listing: This is a view of the Mississippi River and Eads Bridge in St. Louis (Figure 2.10). The picture is half sky and half waterscape. Students can make a three-column chart of all the people, objects, and activities they see. River traffic passes under the bridge and commuter trains pass through the lower level. Students can analyze the activity of the river and discuss its importance as an artery for trade and travel in the 1800s.

Figure 2.10
St. Louis Eads Bridge
Source: The Library of Congress

Assignment: Design a writing activity for students to complete regarding the dust-storm photograph (Figure 2.9) or the Eads Bridge image (Figure 2.10).

Strong Focal-Point Photographs

In a photograph with a strong focal point, the viewer's attention is immediately drawn to one spot. When studying the photograph, that center of attention will need the most emphasis, but the surrounding details can also add meaning. Several teaching strategies can be used for photos with a strong focal point. Students can examine and describe the main action of the focal point and the major characters' parts in the event; examine and describe how the setting enhances the focal point; discuss the emotions the event portrays; and compare this photo event to other similar events.

Analyzing Photographs: These two examples give different ways to use single-focus photographs in the classroom. On the left (Figure 2.11) is the famous photograph of Iwo Jima that set in motion the design of a national statue. The photograph was taken February 23, 1945. This photo's single focal point is the intense effort of these soldiers as they raise the American flag. With this type of photo, students should analyze the soldiers' appearance and the energy of the moment. On another level, students can imagine the emotions of this group as they raised the United States flag and possibly compare this event with other moments when Americans have raised the flag during a time of victory or accomplishment. Students may also want to research information about the photographer and the actual soldiers' lives after the war ended.

Figure 2.11

Flag raising on Iwo Jima
Source: The National Archives

Figure 2.12

Unemployment in America
Source: The National Archives,
Franklin D. Roosevelt Library

In the photo on the right (Figure 2.12), the focal point is a man holding a sign stating his need for a job and not charity. Students can analyze the man's appearance and the sign he is holding. Students might discuss why he is well-dressed rather than in raggedy clothing. Students can also discuss the setting, especially the car on the right side. Eventually, students should realize that this photograph was taken during the Great Depression. Students can compare this photo to one today of a homeless person carrying a sign asking for help.

Assignment: Design a drama-style activity for students to do with one of these strong focal-point photographs. For example, they can reenact the flag-raising scene, attempting the same pose.

Photographs with Multiple Elements

Photographs with multiple elements can be visually divided into quadrants or halves so that students can examine and discuss the setting, people, and objects within each quadrant. Students can also discuss what activity is taking place; guess the date of the famous event in the photograph; or write the questions they have about the scene.

Divided Image: This busy view of New York City's Mulberry Street in 1900 (Figure 2.13) captures many people engaged in various activities. To examine a photograph with this many details, students need to visually divide the photo into quadrants and then examine and list the details within each of the four sections. With young students, teachers should only provide one-fourth of the image to each student to help them focus on only their assigned sections.

A follow-up activity for this type of picture might be to ask student groups to guess the date of the picture by choosing from the dates of 1800, 1865, 1900, or 1925. Groups can try to justify their guesses by citing information from the picture such as the kinds of vehicles that are in the picture; kinds of vehicles not in the picture; types of clothing; and the styles and heights of buildings.

Figure 2.13
Mulberry Street
Source: The Library of Congress

Unlike the Mulberry Street picture, which is an everyday street scene, this Transcontinental Railroad photograph (Figure 2.14) records a famous historic event—joining the East to the West. The crowd was assembled for a purpose. Many historic-event photos also have multiple elements—crowds assembled to watch a presidential speech, protest a cause, participate

in a strike, or fight a battle. For this picture, students can divide this photograph into vertical halves and record what they find: the number of people, the appearance of the clothing, the appearance of each train, the number and location of the workers, and the number and location of the bosses. Students should be asked to conduct research in order to determine how such a significant event affected history and the lives of everyday people.

Assignment: Design an East–West compare and contrast chart for students to complete in order to record their observations for the Transcontinental Railroad photograph. Students can compare the designs of the two trains, the number of people, and more.

Figure 2.14

First Transcontinental Railroad
Source: The National Archives

Photographs of Architectural Structures

Architectural photographs can be of a single item such as a column, a single building, or a grouping of structures. The composition of an architectural photograph may require students to divide the study into foreground and background or study the main parts of the architectural structures such as doorways, embellishments, height, purpose of structure, style, and design. During the study of architectural photographs, students should be introduced to basic architectural terms, such as Doric column, Ionic column, Corinthian column, arch, buttress, steeple, belfry, wings, palladium, and dome.

The amphitheater in Pompeii (Figure 2.15) is very much the main focus of the photograph. In fact, the theater engulfs the entire photo. Examining the amphitheater requires looking for overall details including arches, number of seats, size of the arena, and the purpose of the arena.

The Ruins of Charleston (Figure 2.16) clearly demonstrate the physical destruction war brings. This photograph of the ruins of Charleston can be divided into background and foreground for study.

An interior architectural structure is featured in a room in Independence Hall (Figure 2.17). Since this photograph seems to be symmetrical, studying the two sides of the photograph can provide an opportunity for comparison and contrast of the right and left sides of a photograph.

Figure 2.15

Amphitheater in Pompeii
Source: The Burton Family

Figure 2.16

Ruins of Charleston
Source: The National Archives

Figure 2.17

Interior view of Independence Hall
Source: The Library of Congress

Activity: Write one question for each of these photographs that queries the architectural structures and features.

Photographic Portraits

Photographic portraits have similar characteristics to painted portraits, but they have one specific difference: A painted portrait may have more of the artist's interpretation or may be more flattering than a standard photograph. However, in the age of technology with special lenses and airbrushing techniques, photographers can glamorize and enhance many photographs. Look back at the general questions for painted portraits (page 26) and adapt them to the photographic portraits. Below are three portraits (Figures 2.18, 2.19, and 2.20) to use as examples of different styles of photographic portraits.

The first photograph is a migrant mother from the Great Depression (Figure 2.18). The facial expression of the mother is so intense that it takes a moment to notice the children and other details of the picture. Students viewing this type of photograph should be able to describe the central figure and the surrounding people or details

The second photograph is President Franklin D. Roosevelt during a fireside chat (Figure 2.19). Roosevelt is surrounded by a variety of props that students can describe and some that will cause them to question what an object might be. The person is the focal point, but the setting is of equal interest when studying this type of photo.

Figure 2.18
Migrant Mother
Source: The National Archives,
Franklin D. Roosevelt Library

Figure 2.19
Fireside chat
Source: The National Archives, Franklin D. Roosevelt Library

The third is a drummer boy during the Civil War (Figure 2.20) from when photography was in its infancy. The little drummer boy has a compelling expression, but his clothing and drum are also emphasized in the photograph. Students can discuss the role of a drummer boy in a war. What side of the war did he support? What evidence can you cite?

Figure 2.20
Drummer boy
Source: The National Archives

Assignment: Design a Web search to help students learn about the history behind one of these photographs.

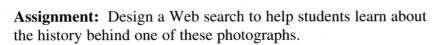

Photographs of Artifacts

Students rarely get the opportunity to hold and examine historic artifacts; therefore, photographs of those objects are frequently used in classroom settings. Pictures of artifacts, either photos or line drawings, are also incorporated on tests. These tests ask students to explain the functions of the items. While these pictures are photographs, in reality they are treated more like a study of artifacts than a study of photography.

Discussion Questions: King Tutankhamen's mask, a Tlingit Totem Pole, and a picture of a very early Apple computer are examples of photographs of artifacts (Figures 2.21, 2.22, and 2.23). The following is a series of questions to consider when studying photographs of objects.

- Describe the artifact and include specific details.
- The photo depicts only one view of a three-dimensional object. What do you think the other sides of this object look like?
- What is the function of the object?
- Who made the object?
- Does the object have any symbolic meaning? If so, what are the symbols and their meanings?
- Why is this artifact important?
- How does this object work? Who would use the object?

Figure 2.21

King Tutankhamen's mask
Source: Courtesy of the Burton Family

Figure 2.22

Tlingit totem pole
Source: Woods Publishing Group

Figure 2.23

Apple computer
Source: Courtesy of Emily R. Smith

Assignment: Design a situation activity for your class featuring one of these artifact pictures. For example, have students pretend that they are the archaeologists who discovered this totem pole. Ask them to describe how they discovered it and what they observed about how it was made.

Prints

Prints include etchings, detailed sketches, book illustrations, illustrated posters, and line drawings. Prints are copies of original paintings or drawings that may have been produced in a limited or unlimited number for political or commercial purposes.

Depending on the style of a print, choose ideas for instruction similar to the previous ones listed for photographs. Below are two examples of prints in the Library of Congress collection. The image on the left is a drawing of the Federal Hall in New York City (Figure 2.24), and the image on the right is a 1914 symbolic poster of Russia portrayed as St. George slaying the dragon, Germany (Figure 2.25).

The "Russia for Justice" poster (Figure 2.25) has symbols that require interpretation. Many prints have symbolic elements that students will need to examine because the symbols are completely unfamiliar to them. Just as the political donkey and elephant are symbols that today's students understand, other eras had their own meaningful symbols. In this case, the St. George image is an allusion to classical literature. Students will need assistance in understanding and interpreting symbols in primary sources from other eras. Teachers can tape a large sheet of chart paper to the classroom wall to list symbols. Students can locate their meanings in primary sources. The chart can then be used as a reference when the students study prints, cartoons, and illustrations throughout the year.

While the Russia illustration provides ample opportunity for discussion and research, the line drawing on the left (Figure 2.24) appears to require little study. However, an inquiring student can formulate questions about the federal hall picture. Where was the federal hall located? Is there still a building called federal hall in New York City? Why was it famous? What is the architecture of this building? What event is being shown in the print?

Figure 2.24
Federal Hall, The Seat of Congress
Source: The Library of Congress

Figure 2.25
Russia for Justice poster
Source: The Library of Congress

Assignment: Write three different levels of questions for the Russia poster: comprehension, application, and analysis.

Model Lessons and Activities

In the final pages of this chapter, three model lessons are provided for using paintings, photographs, and prints. The first lesson is for grades K–3, the second lesson is for grades 4–8, and the final lesson is for grades 9–12. Each lesson provides an image, teaching strategies, and student activity sheet or graphic organizer.

Photograph Model Lesson for Grades K–3

Figure 2.26
Home sewing business
Source: The Library of Congress

Model Lessons and Activities *(cont.)*

Photograph Model Lesson for Grades K–3 *(cont.)*

The photo of the home sewing business (Figure 2.26) is an appropriate photo for this age of students to study because it focuses on the everyday life of another generation—a topic of interest to students in these grade levels. This photo also has a portrait-like quality.

Objectives

- Students will develop an understanding that children 100 years ago frequently spent much of their time involved in work that helped their family survive.

- Students will compare and contrast the lifestyles of this family with their own families.

Teaching Strategies

1. Provide groups of students a copy of the photo on page 35 (Figure 2.26). This photograph is also provided on the CD for your use (filename: sewing.jpg). Let the groups talk for three to five minutes about the photo and share ideas about what they think is happening. Ask each group to share their ideas about the photo with the class.

2. Explain to the students the background of this photo. This is a photo of a family-based sewing business 100 years ago. All four members of this family are working on pieces of material. A company that manufactures clothing gave them these piece goods. These pieces of material were different parts of clothing—sleeves, ruffles, pockets, trim, and cording. When they finished sewing their parts for the clothing, they sent those pieces back to the factory to be made into clothes.

3. Ask the students questions about the people, setting, and activity in the photograph. Here are some examples of types of questions to use with this photograph and other photographs of children from the past.
   - What kind of clothes are the children wearing?
   - Do the clothes look like work clothing or their best clothing?
   - Why do you think they got all dressed up for this photo?
   - How are their clothes different from your clothes?
   - Why did someone take this picture?
   - What do you think each child is doing?
   - Describe the apartment.

4. Give students the graphic organizer (page 37). This graphic organizer can be adjusted to any primary source lesson that requires students to compare living conditions or clothing in a photo with their own living conditions or clothing. Younger students will need someone to help them write what they want to say, while second and third graders should be able to fill in each section of the graphic organizer. Discuss in class what the students have written. Help them understand that children long ago were frequently expected to work to help the family survive and had few toys and no electrical gadgets.

Model Lessons and Activities *(cont.)*

Photograph Model Lesson for Grades K–3 *(cont.)*

Name_____

Comparing My Life with the Lives of Children 100 Years Ago

Their Life	My Life
Their clothes	My clothes
Their living room	My living room/family room
Their chores	My chores
How they spent their day	How I spend my day

Model Lessons and Activities *(cont.)*

Photograph Model Lesson for Grades 4–8

Figure 2.27
Bison hide yard in 1878, Dodge City, Kansas
Source: The National Archives

Background Information

During the building of the Transcontinental Railroad in 1869, the railroad companies authorized the killing of as many bison as needed to keep the construction area clear. Later, they encouraged hunters to ride the trains and shoot bison like ducks in a shooting gallery. Teams of bison hunters also traveled throughout the Plains on wagons. They skinned the bison and took the hides back to camp where they were prepared for shipping. These men usually received $2.00 per hide. The hides were shipped to the East Coast to be made into blankets and rugs. This bison yard has over 40,000 bison hides piled together.

Model Lessons and Activities *(cont.)*

Photograph Model Lesson for Grades 4–8 *(cont.)*

This strong focal-point photograph (Figure 2.27) was chosen as an example because it fits the westward expansion theme, a popular national test category, and offers an interesting subject to discuss.

Objectives

- Students will develop an understanding that during the era of westward expansion, bison were hunted to near extinction due to the efforts of the railroad companies and the hide traders on the East Coast.

- Students will demonstrate an understanding of two points of view by writing a newspaper interview about bison hunting from the perspectives of the professional hunter and an American Indian chief.

Teaching Strategies

1. Place the students in pairs. Provide copies of Figure 2.27 to each group. This photograph is also provided on the CD for your use (filename: bison.jpg). Fold under the background information before giving the photo to students. Tell the students not to look at that information until told to do so. Ask the students to divide the photo in half—left side and right side. Have them list what they see on each side. Ask the students which side is the strong focal point of the photograph. Why? Have them guess how many hides are depicted in this picture. Allow time for students to share their observations with the class.

2. Tell students to unfold and read the information that was written at the bottom of the picture. Ask them to explain how the information changes their ideas about the photo. Require each pair to discuss what they think the man sitting on the hides is doing. Invite the pairs to share their ideas and thoughts with the class in a group discussion.

3. To prepare students for writing interviews about a photograph, provide examples and strategies for writing appropriate questions. Encourage the class members to suggest questions that they would ask someone in the picture or someone who has an opinion about the picture. In this lesson, students must choose to ask questions of a professional bison hunter or an American Indian chief about the amount of hunting illustrated by the picture. Discuss whether they would ask different questions of the American Indian than they would of the bison hunter.

4. Students can work in pairs and pretend that they are a newspaper reporter and a photographer. Using two copies of the *Interview Plan Sheet* (page 40), they can write an interview with the man sitting on the hides, detailing the responsibilities of his job and his opinion of the hide business. The interview must include at least three questions and detailed answers. Each pair will then write an interview with an American Indian chief who lives in a village in the northern Plains region. They should ask him about his feelings regarding the hunting and what this photograph represents. This interview must also have at least three questions and detailed answers.

Model Lessons and Activities *(cont.)*

Photograph Model Lesson for Grades 4–8 *(cont.)*

-- -- -- -- -- -- -- -- -- -- -- -- -- -- -- -- -- -- -- --

Interview Plan Sheet

Name of newspaper: _____

Date of interview: _____

Name of reporter: _____

Name of photographer: _____

Person being interviewed: _____

First Question: _____

Response: _____

_____

_____

Second Question: _____

Response: _____

_____

_____

Third Question: _____

Response: _____

_____

Model Lessons and Activities *(cont.)*

Print Model Lesson for Grades 9–12

Figure 2.28
Eighth Wonder of the World
Source: The Library of Congress

Model Lessons and Activities *(cont.)*

Print Model Lesson for Grades 9–12 *(cont.)*

The Eighth Wonder of the World print (Figure 2.28) was selected for the high-school level because its engaging topic and details are interesting for students to discuss. This multi-faceted print can be used in either a world history or American history class.

Objectives

- Students will demonstrate an understanding that communication across the ocean in the mid-nineteenth century took at least 12 days for mail to go by ship prior to the installation of the Atlantic Cable. This cable reduced the time for messages to 10 hours.

- Students will work with partners to create letters, telegrams, responses, and situational outcomes to demonstrate their understanding of the significant change in communication as a result of the Atlantic Cable.

Teaching Strategies

1. Place students in pairs and ask them to share a magnifying glass or hand lens as they study the print (Figure 2.28). This print is also provided on the CD for your use (filename: cable.jpg).

2. They should answer the following questions regarding the print.

   - What do the following symbols represent: lion, eagle, man with the forked spear, and the two flags?

   - What is the line between the lion and the eagle?

   - What do the four pictures on the corners represent?

   - Where does the cable begin and end?

   - Why would this cable have been called the Eighth Wonder of the World?

   - What were the other seven wonders at this time?

   - From what geographic perspective is this print designed (north, south, east, or west)?

   - Some people say this image seems backwards to them. Why do you think they say this?

3. Students should spend time researching texts and websites about the extensive and expensive process of laying an underwater cable across the Atlantic Ocean as well as the never-give-up attitude of Cyrus Field.

4. Finally, have students work with their partners to create letters, telegram messages, responses, and outcome situations like the example on page 43.

Model Lessons and Activities *(cont.)*

Print Model Lesson for Grades 9–12 *(cont.)*

Name _____

The Transatlantic Cable

The American businessman and adventurer, Cyrus Field, designed, manufactured, and installed the Transatlantic Cable. He conducted five very expensive expeditions between 1857 and 1866, trying to lay the cable on the ocean floor between Newfoundland and Ireland. The first three attempts were failures. The fourth attempt was only a brief success, but allowed a cablegram to be sent between Queen Victoria and President James Buchanan. The fifth attempt (1866) was a huge success because Field had finally developed a technique to make one long cable rather than connecting pieces of cable that could later come apart on the ocean floor. This long cable allowed overseas communication to finally become a routine part of life. How did the telegraph cable change the way people responded to their world when it was first invented? The following is one example of how cablegrams might have changed the world.

Letter received on May 26, 1865

Letter: Sent on May 12, 1865. Dear Lilly, I am so sorry to inform you that your father is gravely ill. I pray you can come in time to be with him in these last days. With deepest sympathy, your cousin, Mary

Response: Mary, I will leave tomorrow on a steamer to London. I'll see you on June 5.

Outcome: If only I had known sooner, I could have been there. When I finally arrived on June 5, I learned my father had died on May 26.

Cablegram received on May 13, 1869

Cablegram: Sent on May 12, 1869. Lilly, Father is very ill. Come be with him in his last days. Mary

Response: Will catch steamer tomorrow. Arrive May 23.

Outcome: I was with my father during his last three days. He died on May 26 knowing that I was with him.

Directions: Design your own letter, response, and outcome as well as telegram, response, and outcome situation. You might send a message about a birth, death, world event, notice of a dangerous disease, or a report about a war or disaster. Use specific dates in your two sets of documents, and check to see if your work is historically accurate.

General Analysis Strategies

Grades K–3

These strategies can be used with any painting, photograph, or print.

- Provide the students with teacher-generated questions about the photo.

- Ask the students to compare and contrast this picture to their own way of life.

- Demonstrate to the students how to use graphic organizers to keep track of their image analysis.

Grades 4–8

These strategies can be used with any painting, photograph, or print.

- Add a fold-under section with background information on the bottom of the page with the photograph. Students read the information only after making certain initial observations about the photo.

- Compare the left side of a photograph to the right side of the same photograph.

- Teach students how to write interview questions, and then have them write both the questions and responses for interviews.

Grades 9–12

These strategies can be used with any painting, photograph, or print.

- Provide students with a magnifying glass or hand lens to examine a historic print, adding a detective quality to the lesson.

- Discuss the symbols represented in the print with the students.

- Engage the students in a conversation about the perspective of a print.

Published Documents and Public Record Documents

Overview

Published documents and public record documents fall into several categories:

- Documents that give insight into the workings of government and businesses or documents that are part of the public record include constitutions, laws, compromises, treaties, acts, court decisions, proclamations, forms, certificates, written versions of speeches, deeds, voting records, immigration records, paper money, and press releases

- Literary documents that include reviews, original poems, plays, published journals, autobiographies, stories, novels, and some newspaper and magazine articles that include personal perspectives

- Posters

- Advertisements

- Scientific documents that include published theories, patents, and results of case studies

- Maps, which will be covered in another section since their graphics require different teaching techniques

Where can one find collections of published and public record documents?

Published and public record documents are found at government agencies, state, county and city archives, business archives, genealogy societies, election boards, Internet sites, family attics and basements, and museums and national institutions such as the Library of Congress and the National Archives. While each presidential library is built with private funding, once built, the National Archives administers the facility and collections. Each presidential library houses the papers of that president and visiting their websites will yield a rich variety of documents for classroom use. (See page 172 for further information on presidential libraries.)

The main holdings of the National Archives and Record Administration are located in Washington, D.C., and in College Park, Maryland. The National Archives also has regional research centers containing a wide variety of documents such as census, federal trial, and American Indian records. Together with other sponsors, the National Archives supports a website (http://www.ourdocuments.gov) that lists 100 milestone documents from American history. Selecting from these documents throughout the study of American history is a wise teaching decision. Seeing images of the original documents of the Bill of Rights, the Articles of Confederation, the Monroe Doctrine, the Emancipation Proclamation, or the Civil Rights Act of 1964 provides important educational moments for students.

The Library of Congress (http://www.loc.gov) contains thousands of digitized documents. To assist teachers and students, the Library of Congress staff developed the American Memory collection on United States history and culture, the Global Gateway about world culture, and a well-organized collection of primary source documents called American Memory Timeline. These are excellent sources for classroom materials, and the suggested teaching resources offer a wide variety of ideas for both historical and cultural studies.

Pages 171–172 have other website resources listed for your reference.

Overview (cont.)

What documents are appropriate for different grade levels?

While most published documents are more appropriate for middle school and high school classrooms, some famous documents such as the Mayflower Compact, the Preamble of the Constitution, the Bill of Rights, the Gettysburg Address, parts of the Louisiana Purchase, and Martin Luther King Jr.'s "I Have a Dream" speech should be introduced in the elementary classroom. Excerpts from other famous speeches such as Patrick Henry's "Give Me Liberty or Give Me Death" speech can be read and interpreted and then reread aloud in an oratory fashion. In addition, students can learn to read official documents such as census records, government-printed posters, and different types of forms.

This image of the Mayflower Compact (Figure 3.1) demonstrates handwriting typical of the era. A typed translation is needed to understand the text and can be obtained by a quick Internet search. Maybe more importantly, students can also read the handwritten copy of the list of passengers who took the long journey. Even young students will enjoy reading about the brave families who risked everything to come to the New World. Many times, it is more important for young students to learn about the history surrounding a document than to read the document itself.

The activities throughout the rest of this chapter will describe ways in which you can analyze documents with your students. An additional list of ideas is provided on pages 56–57.

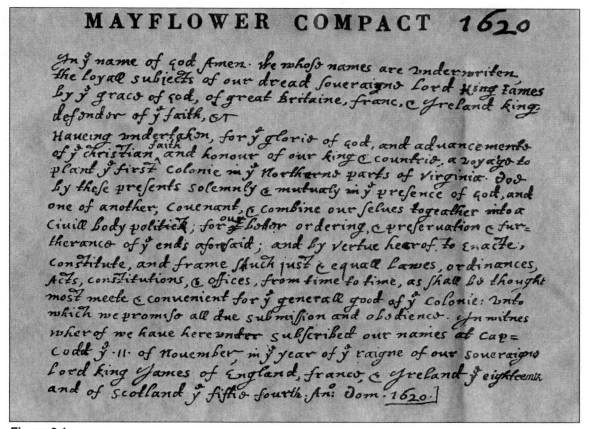

Figure 3.1

Mayflower Compact
Source: Historical Documents, Co.

Signs or Notices

Signs or notices are generally easy documents to read and interpret. Below are two colonial signs (Figures 3.2 and 3.3): one is appropriate for younger elementary students and the other is more appropriate for middle school. In the sign on the left (Figure 3.2), the rules of a tavern are spelled out. Students will enjoy figuring out how these inns were vastly different from hotels today. In the sign on the right (Figure 3.3), a slave auction is advertised. This is a grim reminder that at one time African people, including children, were considered property. Students will notice that of the 94 people being sold, 31 are children. This is a sign that can arouse sensitivity in students when it is analyzed.

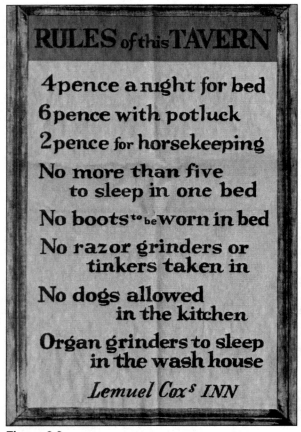

Figure 3.2

Rules of this tavern sign
Source: Historical Documents, Co.

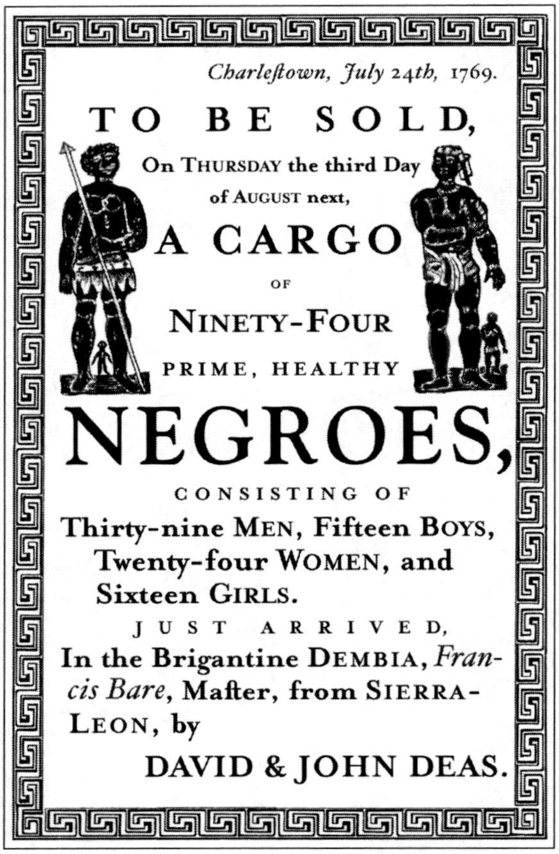

Figure 3.3

Slave auction sign
Source: The Woods Publishing Group

There are some interesting vocabulary words on the tavern sign (Figure 3.2): pence, razor grinders, tinkers, and organ grinders. Possible questions include: How can five people sleep in one bed? Does the four pence per night for a bed mean that it costs four pence per person or four pence for the whole bed? Why were razor grinders or tinkers not allowed in the tavern? Why did organ grinders have to sleep in the washhouse?

Some further points to consider for the slave auction sign (Figure 3.3) are the date and location of the sign, the descriptions of the slaves, and their exact point of origin in Africa. Discuss offensive terms such as calling people "cargo" and the illustrations on the sign. There are ample opportunities with this poster for creative writing and research challenges.

Advertisements

Advertisements are graphic documents focused on persuading the viewer to accept a particular viewpoint or to buy a particular product. Students will probably be experts on this type of published document. They can bring in examples from the mail, newspapers, or magazines. Students can analyze a collection of modern and historic advertisements to sharpen their observation skills. For each advertisement, students can answer the following questions (the same questions can apply to posters):

- What is your first impression of this advertisement/poster? Do you like it? Does it capture your attention? Why or why not?

- Who designed this advertisement/poster?

- Is it easy to understand the point of this advertisement/poster?

- What objects or people are used in this advertisement or poster?

- Are there any symbols or logos? Are they familiar to you? What do they mean?

- What does the graphic artist or creator want you to do, buy, or understand?

These three advertising posters have strong viewpoints. The NAACP poster (Figure 3.4) is campaigning for members. The World War II poster (Figure 3.5) is convincing women that they can carry the workload in the factories. The POW–MIA poster (Figure 3.6) encourages people to remember those who never returned home from the Vietnam War.

Figure 3.4

NAACP membership drive poster
Source: The Woods Publishing Group

Figure 3.5

We Can Do It!
Source: The National Archives

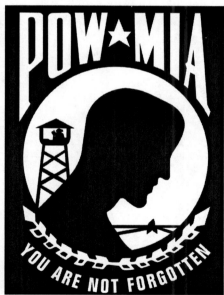

Figure 3.6

POW–MIA symbol
Source: The Woods Publishing Group

Assignment: Pick one question from above for each advertisement poster. Then, write two of your own questions about each poster.

Posters

Posters are good choices for beginning the study of documents. Sometimes posters are a cross between a print and a document, containing visuals that catch the eye.

Historical Research: The James Brothers reward poster (Figure 3.7) will fascinate young students. Students can research to learn why the James brothers were wanted. During research, students will find that writers have either labeled Jesse James a hero or a criminal. Then, students can create modern-day wanted posters. Who would be on the posters? How much money would be offered as a reward?

PROCLAMATION
OF THE
GOVERNOR OF MISSOURI!
$25,000
REWARD
JESSE JAMES
DEAD OR ALIVE
$15,000 REWARD FOR FRANK JAMES
SIGNED ST. LOUIS MIDLAND RAILROAD & STATE OF MISSOURI

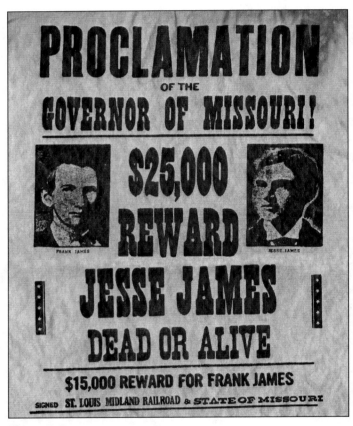

Figure 3.7

Wanted poster for the James brothers

Source: Historical Documents, Co.

Literature Connection: When studying World War II and the Holocaust, a simple poster like the one below (Figure 3.8) can have lots of meanings and implications. This poster works well with books like *The Diary of Anne Frank*, *Escape to Warsaw*, or *Number the Stars.* Ask students if they think this poster was made before the Jewish people were sent to concentration camps or after. Ask them to support their answers with historic facts.

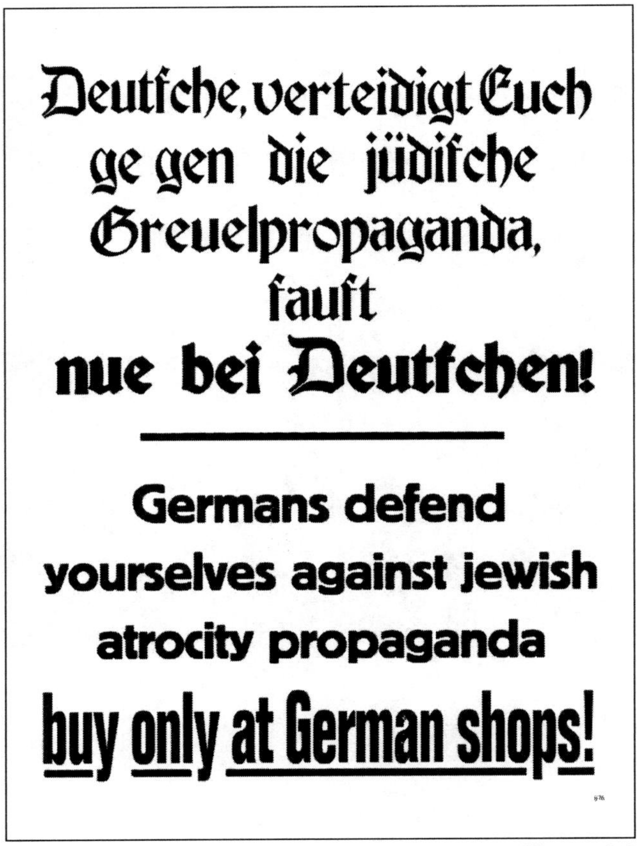

Deutſche, verteidigt Euch
ge gen die jüdiſche
Greuelpropaganda,
kauft
nue bei Deutſchen!
Germans defend
yourselves against jewish
atrocity propaganda
buy only at German shops!

Figure 3.8

German boycott poster

Source: Recreated by Teacher Created Materials

Assignment: Write three questions about one of these posters to promote independent thinking.

Government Forms

Some government documents are forms or vouchers for citizens to use. Blank tax forms are published government documents, but the completed ones are personal. Here are two published documents with different purposes.

The war ration book (Figure 3.9) was printed for citizens to use to buy certain commodities during World War II. Students can study the ration book and learn how citizens were asked to make sacrifices during World War II.

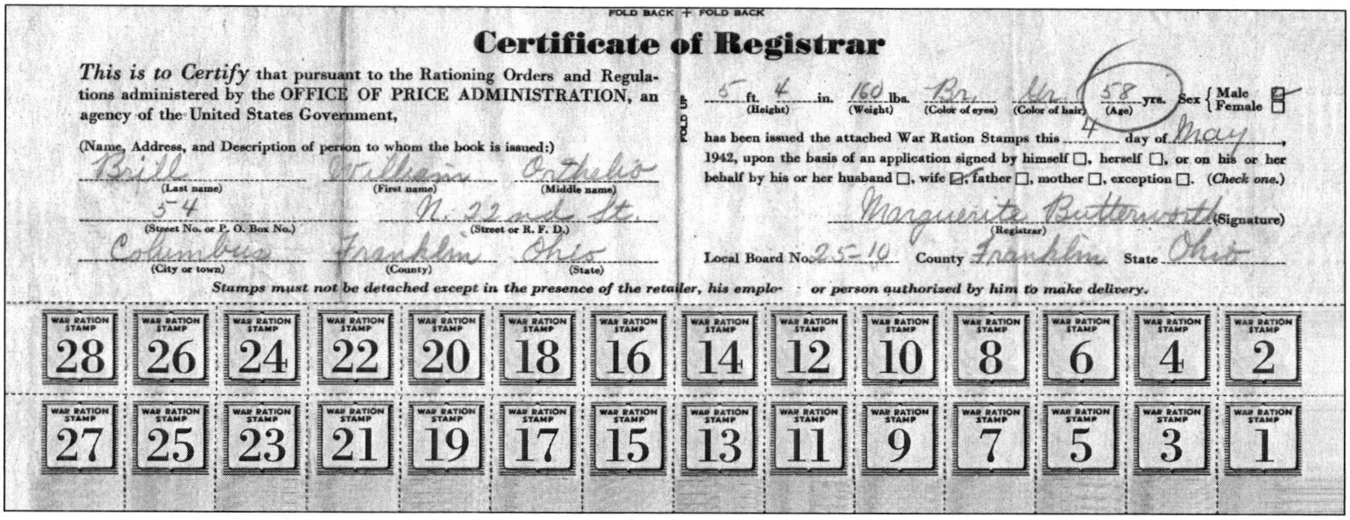

FOLD BACK + FOLD BACK

Certificate of Registrar

This is to Certify that pursuant to the Rationing Orders and Regulations administered by the OFFICE OF PRICE ADMINISTRATION, an agency of the United States Government,

(Name, Address, and Description of person to whom the book is issued:)

Brill (Last name) William (First name) Onthello (Middle name)

54 (Street No. or P. O. Box No.) N. 22nd St. (Street or R. F. D.)

Columbus (City or town) Franklin (County) Ohio (State)

5 ft. 4 in. (Height) 160 lbs. (Weight) Br. (Color of eyes) Gr. (Color of hair) 58 yrs. (Age) Sex { Male / Female }

has been issued the attached War Ration Stamps this 4 day of May, 1942, upon the basis of an application signed by himself ☐, herself ☐, or on his or her behalf by his or her husband ☐, wife ☑, father ☐, mother ☐, exception ☐. (*Check one.*)

Marguerite Butterworth (Registrar) (Signature)

Local Board No. 25-10 County Franklin State Ohio

Stamps must not be detached except in the presence of the retailer, his employe or person authorized by him to make delivery.

WAR RATION STAMP 28, 26, 24, 22, 20, 18, 16, 14, 12, 10, 8, 6, 4, 2

WAR RATION STAMP 27, 25, 23, 21, 19, 17, 15, 13, 11, 9, 7, 5, 3, 1

Figure 3.9
War ration book
Source: The Smith/Mulhall Families

The border permit card (Figure 3.10) depicts a government form pertaining to immigration. The immigration card may be familiar to some students and it may help others to understand how people dream about, plan, and try to come to America for jobs and freedom.

Some questions for both the ration and immigration documents are: What is the purpose of the document? What does it tell us about life in those times? Who used the document? Do we still have documents like this one today? Are there any graphics? What do they mean?

Assignment: Select either the ration book or the immigration document and design a drama activity for your students about the history surrounding the document.

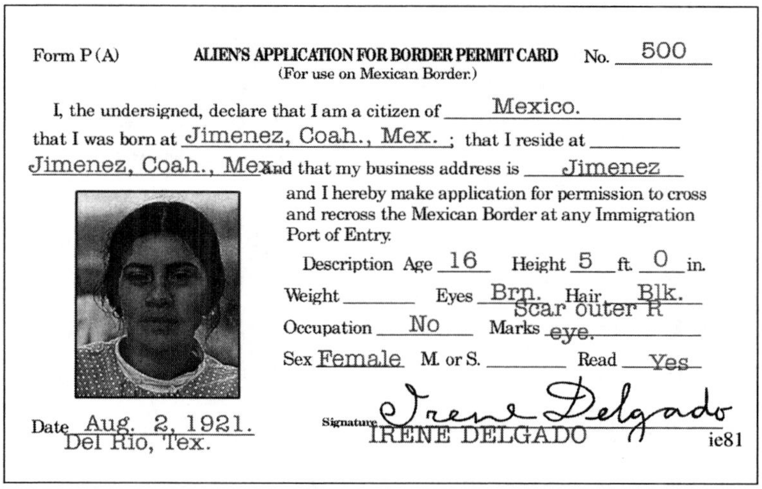

Form P (A) ALIEN'S APPLICATION FOR BORDER PERMIT CARD No. 500
(For use on Mexican Border.)

I, the undersigned, declare that I am a citizen of Mexico. that I was born at Jimenez, Coah., Mex. ; that I reside at Jimenez, Coah., Mex. and that my business address is Jimenez and I hereby make application for permission to cross and recross the Mexican Border at any Immigration Port of Entry.

Description Age 16 Height 5 ft. 0 in.
Weight ____ Eyes Brn. Hair Blk.
Occupation No Marks Scar outer R eye.
Sex Female M. or S. ____ Read Yes

Date Aug. 2, 1921. Del Rio, Tex.

Signature Irene Delgado
IRENE DELGADO ie81

Figure 3.10
Application for border permit card
Source: Immigration and Naturalization Service

Written Published Documents

As aforementioned, most handwritten, published documents and public records are challenging to read and study. Three major issues affect the success students have in studying these published and public-record documents. First, many written published documents have levels of unfamiliar vocabulary, unfamiliar symbols, and archaic writing styles. To further complicate matters, some documents also use Latin or legal jargon. Also, some writing may refer to ideas or activities that are not common today. Second, students may not understand the underlying history leading up to the creation of the document. The document may contain unfamiliar names, places, and situations. Third, a document may have handwriting or images that are difficult to decipher. Therefore, it is important to take document study in phases. In the pages that follow, step-by-step strategies will be explained.

Getting Started

The steps to studying written published and public record documents include:

- Exposing students to different types of documents to view and observe.

- Allowing students to study document excerpts and analyze their content.

- Teaching students how to manage the vocabulary and writing styles found in documents.

- Teaching students summary skills related to document study.

- Teaching students how to analyze a document using a general list and document-specific questions.

- Explaining the historical background of a document or helping students research background information.

- Engaging students in inquiry-based learning activities using documents.

Observation Questions

Bringing a variety of document facsimiles into the classroom for students to view gives them experience in analyzing the various details of a document. Before students read any documents in part or in-depth, they can answer a few questions simply based on surface observations. This perusing activity develops the skill of observation prior to tackling the actual written material.

- What kind of document is this?

- Is there a date?

- Can you tell who wrote the document?

- Does it have a title? Does the title give you a clue about the contents?

- Are there any pictures or images to study?

- What do you think this document will be about?

- Is the document handwritten or typed?

- Is there anything different about the writing that you can observe?

- Does the document have any signatures?

Written Published Documents *(cont.)*

Using Document Excerpts

Most published documents contain long passages, sophisticated language, and difficult vocabulary. Studying government documents or other published materials can be overwhelming for students with little exposure to primary sources or documents. For this reason, and because of time restraints, document excerpts are frequently more practical. Most documents have a key section or two that capture the main essence of the material. When students study those sections, they gain experience working with the vocabulary of document materials and an overall impression of the documents' importance in history. Another practical reason to add document excerpts to your teaching is that excerpts are featured on national and state tests.

One example is this "Go West, Young Man" excerpt from Horace Greeley's editorial in the *New York Tribune*, 1841:

> Do not lounge in the cities! There is room and health in the country, away from the crowds of idlers and imbeciles. Go West, before you are fitted for no life but that of the factory . . . If you have no family or friends to aid you . . . turn your face to the Great West and there build up your home and fortune.

Determining Purpose: This quotation demonstrates persuasive writing, so students can analyze the quote as to what words were chosen and how bias is part of the message. How did a newspaper article like this excite people to travel west? What is the author's point of view? What was the author's purpose for writing this?

Compare and Contrast: Another document excerpt example, Article 29 from the Magna Carta, has a direct tie to the United States Constitution. Asking students to study these lines and find the similar point(s) of law in the Bill of Rights can help students tie our legal heritage to Great Britain's heritage. When studying these few lines, students should consider the meaning of the words *freeman* and *disseised* (a legal term), whether slavery was forbidden, and in what ways a person can be found guilty and punished. Students should be able to identify which amendment(s) in the Bill of Rights is similar to this article in the Magna Carta.

> 29] No Freeman shall be taken, or imprisoned, or be disseised of his Freehold, or Liberties, or free Customs, or be outlawed, or exiled, or any otherwise destroyed; nor will we pass upon him, nor condemn him, but by lawful Judgment of his Peers, or by the Law of the Land. We will sell to no man, we will not deny or defer to any man either Justice or Right.

Assignment: Develop a writing activity for your students from the point of view of an Englishman who knows his Article 29 rights and was just put in prison by a king who refuses to let him have a trial.

Written Published Documents *(cont.)*

Managing the Language

While it is quite acceptable to have students experience a certain level of frustration in trying to decipher a written document's content, it is important to keep students interested in the process and keep them from becoming discouraged. When students work with detailed written documents, they need instruction, not just assignments. The teacher can demonstrate observation techniques and strategies for context clues by using a series of document excerpts prior to assigning longer document-based lessons or assessments.

For example, the opening paragraph to the Declaration of Independence is one long sentence and is quite literary as well as highly persuasive. The words that began the path to independence are not easy for students to read or understand.

> When in the Course of human events, it becomes necessary for one people to dissolve the political bands which have connected them with another, and to assume among the powers of the earth, the separate and equal station to which the Laws of Nature and of Nature's God entitle them, a decent respect to the opinions of mankind requires that they should declare the causes which impel them to the separation.

This style of writing is foreign to students, and the vocabulary is also a challenge. Handing elementary or middle school students even this short paragraph with a set of questions to answer just doesn't work! Students need help wading through the unfamiliar vocabulary, the literary styles, the underlying history, and if handwritten, the style of handwriting.

Style Analysis: When viewing the handwritten copy, students also encounter stylistic letters inserted that make an "s" look like an "f." Students may ask questions like: What does "course of human events" mean? What does "assume among the powers of the earth, the separate and equal station" mean? What words explain why they want to separate from Great Britain? Why do they think they have the right to be independent of Great Britain? Using this type of document requires teacher-student interaction during the elementary and middle school years. By high school, students may be more able to independently analyze documents such as this.

Vocabulary Study: A common vocabulary strategy is for the teacher to make a vocabulary list prior to students reading the document. The list can be written on the board, on an overhead transparency, or reproduced on paper. Students can look for words on the list as the document is read aloud. Furthermore, you can strengthen your students' vocabulary skills by posting a document word-list. Attach a large sheet of poster paper to the wall and entitle it *Document Words to Know*. List key vocabulary and brief definitions of words you encounter in the texts. As students study documents from a certain unit, add words that you or they think should be included in this chart.

Written Published Documents *(cont.)*

Managing the Language *(cont.)*

Vocabulary Study: Give each student a copy of a document excerpt, like the one at the bottom of this page. Have students determine the number of sentences in the excerpt. (Often historic manuscripts have fewer sentences in them than we might use today. There are only two sentences in the excerpt from the Magna Carta below.) Discuss why they think many words are capitalized even when they are not proper nouns. (This was a technique that early writers used to emphasize the importance of certain words.)

Assign someone to read aloud the first sentence while other students highlight or underline on their copies the words they do not understand. Go back through the sentence and have students name the first word that was not understood, then the second, etc. As each word is identified, have students use the context clues or substitute a familiar word to see if the sentence makes sense.

Explain to students that English word usage has changed over time and that there are many phrases that seem awkward to us today. Some words may require dictionary definitions. For example, students will need to look up *intreated* and decide which definition fits the context. The word *Tolts* is probably not found in the dictionary, but it is found on the Internet as a term for a horse gait or a Russian term . . . neither of which fit this context. Going through this vocabulary process and admitting that even teachers get stumped about the meaning of some archaic words, shows students that document research can be like trying to solve a puzzle.

The Magna Carta article #30 focuses on laws pertaining to merchants.

30] All Merchants (if they were not openly prohibited before) shall have their safe and sure Conduct to depart out of England, to come into England, to tarry in, and go through England, as well by Land as by Water, to buy and sell without any manner of evil Tolts, by the old and rightful Customs, except in Time of War. And if they be of a land making War against us, and such be found in our Realm at the beginning of the Wars, they shall be attached without harm of body or goods, until it be known unto us, or our Chief Justice, how our Merchants be intreated there in the land making War against us; and if our Merchants be well intreated there, theirs shall be likewise with us.

Written Published Documents *(cont.)*

Higher-Level Strategies

Obviously you may want to skip or just quickly review the vocabulary and context-clues steps for high school students. Depending on the reading levels of your students, you can proceed directly to the complete document analysis. However, students should still summarize and paraphrase parts of the document to demonstrate their understanding. Giving students ample experience responding to document excerpts is also a wise strategy since they will encounter excerpts on standardized testing.

High school students should be working at higher levels of thinking. Application, analysis, synthesis, and evaluation questions and tasks need to be included. Here are several general strategies you may want to use with your more advanced students.

- After reading the first few sentences of the document, have students predict what information the document will include. Students then read to see if their predictions were accurate.

- As students read each section, they write questions they have about the section, they write why that section is important to us today, or they write why the section no longer applies today.

- Divide the document into parts. Assign pairs of students to teach their parts to the class in a creative way.

- Students compare and contrast ideas in one document with ideas in another document.

- Students describe who the author is and why he/she/they wrote the document.

- Students describe what risks the person took in writing this document?

- Students evaluate how history would have been different if this document had not been written.

- Students answer this question. Did the action that occurred because of this document affect any other cultures? If so, how?

- Students analyze who would have been opposed to this document and explain their answers.

- Students debate the two sides of the issue contained within the document.

- Students write whether they would have supported or disliked the document if they had lived in that era.

Analyzing a Complete Document

Provide students with a facsimile of a complete document. They will examine the aspects of the whole document rather than the content of just a portion or excerpt. Once again, students need instruction, guidance, and group work prior to working with complete documents independently. After students are comfortable with the process, they can work individually or in pairs to analyze other documents. It is not enough for students to answer the questions such as those on page 57—they need to find evidence in the text to support their answers. That is the tricky part! If you approach this type of activity together as a detective's adventure of finding clues, you will have a much more receptive audience of learners.

Written Published Documents *(cont.)*

Generic Questions to Use with Any Document

Here is a list of questions that apply to most document formats. Some of the questions can also be used during the stages of observation. However, when students analyze a complete document, they are not just observing: they are reading, finding answers, and supporting those answers with details.

- What type of document is this?

- Who wrote it?

- Why did the person write the document?

- What is the author's point of view?

- When was the document written?

- Who is the audience for this document?

- What are the most important things about this document?

- Are there any clues about how life was different when this document was written from life today?

- What question would you like to ask this author?

- What are some unanswered questions based on this document?

- If this document had not been written, would the world be different today?

You can also prepare a list of questions for the document that students can answer regarding the specific meanings of the different sections. Or, you could create an anticipation guide for the students to complete. Your anticipation guide should have 5–10 statements on it. Before looking at the document, students determine whether or not they believe the statements are true or false. Then, they use the document to go back and check their predictions about the statements. This is a great way to help focus your students on the five or so most important details from the document.

After working together to analyze several documents and answer the generic questions, students should gain enough confidence for you to start making document detective-work a frequent part of class assignments. You can provide examples of documents or excerpts on the overhead projector or as desk copies when students first enter the room. Give students time to look over the document and to answer some of the basic questions listed above. Next, the students can list people, places, words, and ideas that they think are important. Also, they can each write a question they would like to ask about the document. Thus, the inquiry process begins.

Inquiry Process

The inquiry process involves inviting students to study a document, not only from the point of view of what the document says and means, but also from the perspective of what else the student wants to know about the document. Inquiring minds want to know!

Asking Questions: After studying the NAACP poster (Figure 3.4 on page 49), students may want to know more about the organization. After studying the "freeman" excerpt of the Magna Carta (page 53), students may want to know why the article talks about freemen but not about making people slaves. If there are no slaves, then how can there be freemen? Were there slaves in Great Britain? Or does the word *freemen* mean something different? Will students find all the answers to their questions? No, but they will be able to analyze sources more deeply from having asked the questions. They may choose as a class to take one or two questions and act as detectives to find the answers.

Here are some inquiry-style questions to help get students started. Please note that the best questions come from the students' own curiosity about the document and the people it affected.

- What happened to the people who wrote this document?

- Why did they write this document?

- Who opposed this document being written?

- What happened on the day this document was signed or published?

- How would I feel about this document if I lived back when it was written?

- Does this document contain a mystery?

- Who were the people who handwrote official documents long ago? What happened when they made mistakes?

- How was this document published? Handwritten, printed on a hand press, printed on a machine, posted on the Internet, and so on?

- How are government documents published today?

Assignment: Write three inquiry questions regarding this World War I advertisement (Figure 3.11).

NOTICE!

   TRAVELLERS intending to embark on the Atlantic voyage are reminded that a state of war exists between Germany and her allies and Great Britain and her allies; that the zone of war includes the waters adjacent to the British Isles; that, in accordance with formal notice given by the Imperial German Government, vessels flying the flag of Great Britain, or any of her allies, are liable to destruction in those waters and that travellers sailing in the war zone on ships of Great Britain or her allies do so at their own risk.

IMPERIAL GERMAN EMBASSY
WASHINGTON, D. C.,   APRIL 22, 1915

Figure 3.11
German advertisement from 1915
Source: *The New York Times*

Model Lessons and Activities

In the final pages of this chapter, four model lessons are provided for using published and public record documents. The first two lessons are for grades 4–8 and the second two lessons are for grades 9–12. Each lesson provides a document and teaching strategies.

Published Document Model Lesson 1 for Grades 4–8

Figure 3.12
Lincoln election poster from 1860
Source: The National Archives

Model Lessons and Activities *(cont.)*

Published Document Model Lesson 1 for Grades 4–8 *(cont.)*

Objectives

- Students will learn about the election of 1860 and Abraham Lincoln's campaign. They will apply that knowledge to Lincoln's second campaign in 1864.
- Students will design a banner reflecting Lincoln's 1864 campaign.

Teaching Strategies

1. Students will work as partners to analyze the election banner (Figure 3.12). This document is also provided on the CD for your use (filename: election.jpg).

2. Have students answer the following questions:
   - What is the purpose of this document?
   - Why did the designer change Lincoln's name to Abram and not to Abe? (Abram was the biblical name of Abraham, so Abram is another nickname or shortened version of the name Abraham. Abram became the father of Israel. Therefore, the name suggests Lincoln will play a similar role for America).
   - How was the poster designed to hang? Why did the designer want it to hang that way?
   - Why did the designer use a flag theme?
   - How many stars are in the circle around Lincoln? Is the number of stars significant?

3. Share the following background information with the students.

   In the 1860 presidential campaign, propaganda was actively used to promote candidates. This poster supports the candidacy of Abraham Lincoln during his first presidential campaign. The Republican Party met in Chicago and chose Lincoln as their presidential candidate and Hannibal Hamlin from Maine as the vice presidential candidate.

4. Student groups will research both the 1860 and 1864 elections and answer these questions:
   - Who was the vice-presidential candidate in 1864? Why was it not Hamlin?
   - What was different about the 1864 campaign and the 1860 campaign? What was happening in the United States at that time?
   - What were the biggest issues in the 1860 election? What were the biggest issues in the 1864 election?

5. Using large white construction paper, markers, a picture of Lincoln, and colored construction paper, have students assume the role of banner designers. They must construct new banner-style posters for Lincoln to use in the 1864 election. Lincoln wants a similar design to the 1860 banner that features some kind of patriotic or flag format. However, remember that things are vastly different in 1864 than they were four years earlier Changes in symbols, numbers of stars, and names may be needed. A slogan may also be needed.

Model Lessons and Activities *(cont.)*

Published Document Model Lesson 2 for Grades 4–8

Massaoit was born around 1590 and was known as Yellow Feather. At the time the Pilgrims landed in Plymouth, he was 30 years old and the leader of the Wampanoag tribe. Eventually he decided to meet the settlers and accepted their gifts presented by Edward Winslow. Winslow told Massaoit that he sent greetings to their tribe in the name of the king of Great Britain. Massasoit was impressed and thought an alliance with these settlers might be a good idea since they had the backing of a powerful king. When the settlers pushed for a peace treaty, Massasoit agreed. On March 22, 1621, both groups signed a treaty that lasted 50 years. Below is an account of the treaty.

Treaty of Massasoit

. . . the coming of their great Sachem, called Massasoit. Who, about four or five days after, came with the chief of his friends and other attendance, with the aforesaid Squanto. With whom, after friendly entertainment and some gifts given him, they made a peace with him (which hath now continued this 24 years) in these terms:

I. That neither he nor any of his, should injure or do hurt to any of their people.

II. That if any of his did any hurt to any of theirs, he should send the offender that they might punish him.

III. That if any thing were taken away from any of theirs, he should cause it to be restored; and they should do the like to his.

IV. That if any did unjustly war against him, they would aid him; and if any did war against them, he should aid them.

V. That he should send to his neighbours confederates to certify them of this, that they might not wrong them, but might be likewise comprised in the conditions of peace.

VI. That when their men came to them, they should leave their bows and arrows behind them.

Recorded in *Of Plymouth Plantation* by William Bradford

Source: Pilgrim Hall Museum

Model Lessons and Activities *(cont.)*

Published Document Model Lesson 2 for Grades 4–8 *(cont.)*

Objectives

- Students will understand the historical background of the 1621 treaty between the Separatists (Pilgrims) and Massasoit, leader of the Wampanoag tribe.

- Students will analyze the parts of the Wampanoag/Pilgrim peace treaty as to the benefits of the treaty for each side.

Teaching Strategies

1. Students will read the account of the treaty (page 61 excerpt) and background information with a partner. Students should underline parts they do not understand.

2. They will then answer the following questions:

   - What kind of document is this?

   - What is the purpose of this document?

   - Who recorded the document in his journal?

   - Why was this document important to both the Wampanoag tribe and the Separatists (Pilgrims)?

3. Meet as a class to discuss the students' answers to the questions and the parts of the excerpt that they did not understand. Talk about the main points of the treaty. Ask students to describe which points they think were most important?

4. Students should next work with partners to decide which points of the treaty helped the Pilgrims, which points helped the Wampanoag tribe, and which points helped both. By each statement, students will put the letter that matches the group(s) that most benefited: P=Pilgrim, W=Wampanoag tribe, and B=both. Meet together as a class to compare answers. Which group seemed to benefit most from the treaty?

Extension Activity

Students can write a classroom letter to the Seaconke Wampanoag tribe asking them to send pamphlets or other information about their tribe. Choose one person to type the letter on the computer and have all of the members of the class sign it. Make sure students thank the tribe in writing if they receive any information.

Model Lessons and Activities *(cont.)*

Published Document Model Lesson 1 for Grades 9–12

While this is a personal journal, it was written with the intention of being an official record of the establishment of the first colony. Bradford expected it to be used by historians and eventually published. Therefore, it can be studied as a public record document rather than a personal document.

The "Starving Time" of Early 1621

In these hard & difficulte beginings they found some discontents & murmurings arise amongst some, and mutinous speeches & carriags in other; but they were soone quelled & overcome by ye wisdome, patience, and just & equall carrage of things by ye Govr and better part, wch clave faithfully togeather in ye maine. But that which was most sadd & lamentable was, that in 2. or 3. moneths time halfe of their company dyed, espetialy in Jan: & February, being ye depth of winter, and wanting houses & other comforts; being infected with ye scurvie & other diseases, which this long vioage & their inacomodate condition had brought upon them; so as ther dyed some times 2. or 3. of a day, in ye foresaid time; that of 100. & odd persons, scarce 50. remained. And of these in ye time of most distres, ther was but 6. or 7. sound persons, who, to their great comendations be it spoken, spared no pains, night nor day, but with abundance of toyle and hazard of their owne health, fetched them woode, made them fires, drest them meat, made their beads, washed their lothsome cloaths, cloathed & uncloathed them; in a word, did all ye homly & necessarie offices for them wch dainty & quesie stomacks cannot endure to hear named; and all this willingly & cherfully, without any grudging in ye least, shewing herein their true love unto their friends & bretheren. A rare example & worthy to be remembred. Two of these 7. were Mr. William Brewster, ther reverend Elder, & Myles Standish, ther Captein & military comander, unto whom my selfe, & many others, were much beholden in our low & sicke condition.

Recorded in *Of Plymouth Plantation* by William Bradford
Source: Pilgrim Hall Museum

Model Lessons and Activities *(cont.)*

Published Document Model Lesson 1 for Grades 9–12 *(cont.)*

Objectives

- Students will study the historical background of the starving time of the Plymouth colony and what obstacles the colonists had to overcome during the first winter.

- Students will analyze the old English writing utilized in the Bradford journal entry, paraphrase sections, and answer comprehension questions about the text.

Teaching Strategies

1. Distribute copies of the document (page 63). Ask students to examine the document and answer the following questions:

   - What type of document is this?
   - Who wrote it, and why did the person write the document?
   - When was the document written?
   - Who is the audience for this document?
   - What are the most important things about this document?
   - Are there any clues about how life was different when this document was written than life is today?
   - What question would you like to ask this author?

2. This document is an entry from William Bradford's diary, *Of Plymouth Plantation*, and describes the first winter in the Plymouth colony. The old English in the document is provided for the students. Students may struggle to read it, but in some ways, the activity will be an adventure. Students can understand what reading an original "old-English" document is like for historians. The document is double-spaced so that students can write modern words above the old English words that need interpretation. The first part of this assignment for students will be to work in partners to read the text. As they read, ask students to write modern words above the old English words when required for understanding.

3. Place the pairs of students into groups of four. They should discuss the changes each pair made, and then reread the document aloud.

4. Finally, have students work individually to answer the questions on the *William Bradford Journal Analysis* activity sheet (page 65).

Enrichment Activity

Use the Internet to find out which Pilgrims did not survive the first year. Did more women or more men die? How well did the children survive the winter? What seems to be the main cause of death? Compare this list to the original Mayflower list to see who survived the first year.

Model Lessons and Activities *(cont.)*

Published Document Model Lesson 1 for Grades 9–12 *(cont.)*

Name_____

William Bradford Journal Analysis

Directions: Answer the following questions about the Bradford journal entry that describes the starving time in Plymouth.

1. Paraphrase in 12 words or less the basic meaning of the first sentence.

   _____

   _____

2. Which were the hardest months in the colony? Support your answer with a quotation from the text.

   _____

   _____

3. How many people actually survived the winter? Approximately what percentage of the original settlers remained?

   _____

4. On average, how many people were available to take care of the sick and dying?

   _____

5. Was William Bradford ill during this time? Support your answer using details from the text.

   _____

   _____

6. What are at least two patterns of spelling in old English that are different from today?

   _____

   _____

   _____

7. On another piece of paper, agree or disagree with the following statement by using supportive details: *People today do not have the charity and stamina to withstand a winter like the Separatists in the Plymouth colony experienced during the winter of 1621.*

Model Lessons and Activities *(cont.)*

Published Document Model Lesson 2 for Grades 9–12

Establishing the President's Committee on Equality of Treatment and Opportunity in the Armed Forces

WHEREAS it is essential that there be maintained in the armed services of the United States the highest standards of democracy, with equality of treatment and opportunity for all those who serve in our country's defense:

NOW THEREFORE, by virtue of the authority vested in me as President of the United States, by the Constitution and the statutes of the United States, and as Commander in Chief of the armed services, it is hereby ordered as follows:

1. It is hereby declared to be the policy of the President that there shall be equality of treatment and opportunity for all persons in the armed services without regard to race, color, religion or national origin. This policy shall be put into effect as rapidly as possible, having due regard to the time required to effectuate any necessary changes without impairing efficiency or morale.

2. There shall be created in the National Military Establishment an advisory committee to be known as the President's Committee on Equality of Treatment and Opportunity in the Armed Services, which shall be composed of seven members to be designated by the President.

3. The Committee is authorized on behalf of the President to examine into the rules, procedures and practices of the Armed Services in order to determine in what respect such rules, procedures and practices may be altered or improved with a view to carrying out the policy of this order. The Committee shall confer and advise the Secretary of Defense, the Secretary of the Army, the Secretary of the Navy, and the Secretary of the Air Force, and shall make such recommendations to the President and to said Secretaries as in the judgment of the Committee will effectuate the policy hereof.

4. All executive departments and agencies of the Federal Government are authorized and directed to cooperate with the Committee in its work, and to furnish the Committee such information or the services of such persons as the Committee may require in the performance of its duties.

5. When requested by the Committee to do so, persons in the armed services or in any of the executive departments and agencies of the Federal Government shall testify before the Committee and shall make available for use of the Committee such documents and other information as the Committee may require.

6. The Committee shall continue to exist until such time as the President shall terminate its existence by Executive order.

Executive Order 9981 by Harry Truman, July 26, 1948
Source: Truman Presidential Library and Museum

Model Lessons and Activities *(cont.)*

Published Document Model Lesson 2 for Grades 9–12 *(cont.)*

Objectives

- Students will understand the historical background of the Executive Order: Establishing the President's Committee on Equality of Treatment and Opportunity in the Armed Forces. And, they will understand what were the important implications of this order to minorities in the United States of America.

- Students will analyze Executive Order 9981 and be able to list the important aspects of the document and how the order was designed to be successful.

Teaching Strategies

1. Read aloud this brief history of Executive Order 9981, or read more detailed information from another source.

   During World War II, African Americans fought bravely in all fronts and in all areas of the military—but in separate divisions. Civil Rights activists and President Harry S. Truman felt that this segregation policy was wrong and sought ways to integrate the armed forces. Thus, President Truman decided to appoint a President's Committee on Civil Rights in December 1946. On October 29, 1947, the Committee on Civil Rights presented its report condemning segregation wherever it existed and specifically criticized segregation in the armed forces. Truman decided the process would be too long and complicated to get a law through Congress supporting desegregation of the armed forces. Because the armed forces fall under the supervision of the president as commander in chief, Truman decided to issue his own order. In January 1948, President Truman ended segregation in the armed forces and the civil service through administrative action rather than through legislation. The process took several months and numerous meetings with military personnel. On July 26, 1948, in the midst of the presidential-election campaign, President Truman signed Executive Order 9981, which states, "It is hereby declared to be the policy of the President that there shall be equality of treatment and opportunity for all persons in the armed services without regard to race, color, religion, or national origin." The order also established the President's Committee on Equality of Treatment and Opportunity in the Armed Services.

2. Require groups of students to read the Executive Order (page 66) and discuss the main points. The document is straight-forward with no flowery phrases. It specifically "orders" what must be accomplished. Ask students to work in groups to discuss the tone of the order.

3. Finally, have students individually complete the *Executive Order 9981* activity sheet (page 68).

Enrichment Activity

Research and report on how this order changed Colin Powell's life.

Model Lessons and Activities *(cont.)*

Published Document Model Lesson 2 for Grades 9–12 *(cont.)*

Name_____

Executive Order 9981

Directions: Answer the following questions about President Truman's order to desegregate the armed forces.

1. List the verbs in this document that are "orders."

   _____

   _____

2. What steps did Truman take in this document to ensure that his orders would be carried out and that there would be a way to check for compliance?

   _____

   _____

   _____

3. What is the role of the President's Committee on Equality of Treatment and Opportunity in the Armed Services? Who might appreciate the work of this committee and who might be concerned about the work of this committee?

   _____

   _____

   _____

4. Why was a section added that refers to calling people to testify? Why would that section be needed?

   _____

   _____

5. Choose one of the following activities to complete:

   - Write a well-constructed letter to President Truman congratulating him for this decision. Provide details to support your agreement with his decision.
   - Write a well-constructed paragraph describing how this order led the way for more opportunities for minorities. Provide details to support your ideas.

General Analysis Strategies

Historical Background

Many times students do not know the underlying history leading up to the creation of a document, so the teacher will either need to provide the background information or have students conduct some research to find the "history" behind the historical document. Time constraints may require that you just give students the historical background of the document and explain how the document ties into what they are currently studying. However, inquiry-based learning—where students find the answers to questions they have generated about a document—is certainly worth the time and effort whenever possible.

Quick Review

During the study of official documents students can:

- observe different kinds of documents to become familiar with their styles and surface content.

- become familiar with vocabulary words that occur in documents.

- learn how to use context clues and substitute words they think might fit in place of words they do not know.

- look up meanings of unfamiliar words and choose the correct meanings.

- add document vocabulary words to a word chart.

- paraphrase, restate, tell in their own words, and summarize the context of document passages.

- answer a series of generic questions about a whole document, supporting their responses with quotations from the text.

- make lists of names, places, and ideas they find in a document.

- receive or research historical background information about the document to understand its place and purpose in history.

- generate a list of questions they want to know about the document and learn to research for answers, when time permits.

- role-play or dramatize the events surrounding a document.

- recreate documents (especially posters and advertisements) from the past using content and symbols of today.

General Analysis Strategies *(cont.)*

Follow-up Assignments

As students become familiar with document study, they can be assigned tasks, writing prompts, and creative projects related to documents. The following are some examples of ideas to try in the classroom with a variety of official documents. Students can:

- design an Internet scavenger hunt about the history behind the document.

- debate the major topic of the document from two sides. For example, was the Emancipation Proclamation a moral document or a political document?

- write an editorial for a newspaper of the time period supporting the ideas in the document with examples and details.

- construct a graphic, grid, or chart to summarize the important points of the document.

- write an interview with the author of the document. Include both interviewer's questions and the author's responses.

- develop a timeline of the events leading up to the writing or construction of the document.

- write a character portrayal of the person or people who used the document. This could apply to forms, receipts, memos, daily schedules, ration books, and so on.

- design and present a skit regarding the important events of the document.

- write an answer to a letter that was written by assuming the role of the person the letter was written to originally.

- write a telegram about the historic event of the document as if you had witnessed the event.

- construct a cause-and-effect chart about the document.

- write a set of true and false questions about the contents and the time period of the document to give to another pair of students to answer.

- prepare a multimedia presentation on the topic featured in the document.

- design a persuasive poster about the information in the document.

- create a crossword puzzle or word search of the vocabulary words significant to the document.

- design a pamphlet detailing the information in the document and the events surrounding it.

- write and present a two-minute speech about the contents of the document—supporting or refuting the ideas it contains.

Unpublished Documents and Personal Documents

Overview

Everyone has their own unpublished and personal documents. Unlike published and public record documents, these items were never intended for public distribution. So, it is obviously a bit more difficult to find documents within this category from historical periods. As you read through this section of the book, you may want to refer back to the previous chapter quite often. Many of the suggestions and strategies described for published and public record documents would work just as well for unpublished and personal documents.

Unpublished and personal documents fall into several categories:

- letters, postcards, telegrams, e-mails, diaries, journals, memos, agendas, daily schedules, school papers, unpublished first drafts of stories or books

- recipes, family biographies, scrapbooks, family Bibles

- marriage licenses, deeds to property, wills, military ID cards, birth certificates, baptismal certificates, architectural drawings, land surveys, blueprints, research files, bills, cancelled checks

Where can one find unpublished and personal documents?

While unpublished and personal documents are mostly found in private homes, schools, or businesses, it is possible to find many personal documents at state, county, and city archives; genealogy societies; Internet sites; museums; and national institutions such as the Library of Congress and the National Archives. Families may donate collections of letters, diaries, journals, and other personal materials to a local archives or a national museum with the hope that these documents will give insight into the lives and thoughts of people during a certain era or of people experiencing a historic event such as a war. Make time to see what unique unpublished documents you can find in your area museums and archives.

The National Archives and the Library of Congress have collections of unpublished and personal documents as well as published and public record documents. Some of their collections focus on everyday life. Letters from soldiers are part of their collections and the collections of many museums. Even presidents have collections of personal papers that were never entered into public record. Presidential personal papers make interesting reading, and many letters, daily schedules, memos, and meeting agendas can be accessed at presidential library websites.

Students can actually look through their own desks to get some examples of unpublished documents— school papers, report cards, notes from friends, activity sheets generated by the teacher, phone messages, handwritten notes from parents, or weekly lunch schedules. It might be a good exercise to determine which items in the room are published and which are unpublished documents. Are the weekly newsletters or menus published or unpublished documents? Does *published* mean for everyone or just for a certain audience? Discussions like these stimulate student thinking and help them understand that everything does not fit neatly into categories. Some things are open for interpretation.

Teaching with Unpublished Documents

Teaching with unpublished documents is similar to teaching with published documents. Unpublished and personal documents from centuries prior to the twentieth century can still have difficult phrasings and formal language for students to encounter. Overall, unpublished documents allow for an easier and more relaxed reading for students. They are more personal. Sometimes, it feels as if you are snooping into the private lives of people from long ago. To help students effectively study unpublished documents, use the following list of the strategies. Many of these strategies were covered in detail in the chapter on Published Documents and Public Record Documents (pages 45–70).

Examining Unpublished Documents

During the study of unpublished documents it is important for students to:

- observe different kinds of documents to become familiar with their styles and surface content.
- become familiar with vocabulary words that occur in documents.
- learn how to use context clues and substitute words they think might fit in place of words they do not know.
- look up meanings of unfamiliar words and choose the correct meanings.
- add document vocabulary words to a word chart.
- paraphrase, restate, tell in their own words, and summarize the context of document passages.
- answer a series of generic questions about a whole document, supporting their responses with quotations from the text.
- make lists of names, places, and ideas they find in a document.
- receive or research historical background information about the document to understand its place and purpose in history.
- generate a list of questions they want to know about the document and learn to research for answers, when time permits.
- role-play or dramatize the events surrounding a document.
- recreate documents (especially posters and advertisements) from the past using content and symbols of today.

General Questions

The following list is similar to that used with published documents with a few changes to accommodate the more personal side of unpublished documents.

- What type of document is this, and when was it written?
- Who wrote it, and why did the person write the document?
- What clues about the author's life are found in this document?
- Who is the audience for this document?
- What are the most important things about this document?
- Are there any clues about how life was different when this document was written from life today?
- How do you think this author would feel about having this document read by other people?
- What question(s) would you like to ask this author?

Documents to Use with Young Students

In some cases, unpublished documents are somewhat easier to read than published documents. However, historic letters often include elaborate writing styles that make them difficult for elementary students to decipher. The content will also determine the suitability of a document. For example, the diaries of women on the Oregon Trail give students insight into the difficulties of daily life in a wagon train. And, they consist of appropriate language and subject matter for young students.

Here is an excerpt of the text of a letter written by Narcissa Whitman to her sister. The Whitmans traveled west to establish an Indian mission. The letter was written while the family was traveling west and is not too difficult to read.

Platte River, just above the Forks

June 3rd, 1836.

Dear Sister Harriet and Brother Edward:

Friday eve, six o'clock. We have just encamped for the night near the bluffs over against the river. The bottoms are a soft, wet plain, and we were obliged to leave the river yesterday for the bluffs. The face of the country yesterday afternoon and today has been rolling sand bluffs, mostly barren, quite unlike what our eyes have been satiated with for weeks past. No timber nearer than the Platte, and the water tonight is very bad—got from a small ravine. We have usually had good water precious to this.

Our fuel for cooking since we left timber (no timber except on rivers) has been dried buffalo dung; we now find plenty of it and it answers a very good purpose, similar to the kind of coal used in Pennsylvania (I suppose now Harriet will make up a face at this, but if she was here she would be glad to have her supper cooked at any rate in this scarce timber country). The present time in our journey is a very important one. The hunter brought us buffalo meat yesterday for the first time. Buffalo were seen today but none have been taken. We have some for supper tonight. Husband is cooking it—no one of the company professes the art but himself. I expect it will be very good. Stop—I have so much to say to the children that I do not know in what part of my story to begin. I have very little time to write. I will first tell you what our company consists of. We are ten in number; five missionaries, three Indian boys and two young men employed to assist in packing animals . . . .

Assignment: Find this entire letter or another letter from a woman on the pioneer trails on the Internet. Choose three more paragraphs that you think might interest your students and add those excerpts to the two above for students to read and analyze. Develop a set of questions for each paragraph.

Documents to Use with Young Students *(cont.)*

Another type of official document that is appropriate in the elementary classroom is a president's daily schedule. A president's daily schedule will intrigue students and enable them to compare their day with a president's day. These schedules can be accessed at most presidential library websites.

Below is an excerpt from President Gerald Ford's diary dated April 28, 1975. The full diary is available at his library's website. This excerpt begins in the afternoon and ends in the evening with the president not yet having eaten dinner. Studying the excerpt will help students to understand how busy a president's day can be. Ask students to compare their afternoon and evening with President Ford's. Upper-level students might be interested to see some familiar names on this list.

2:03–2:26	The President met with Secretary of Health, Education, and Welfare (HEW) Caspar W. Weinberger.
2:30–3:16	The President met with: Mr. Rumsfeld, Richard B. Cheney, Deputy Assistant
3:50–3:56	The President participated in the swearing-in ceremony of John Dellenback as Associate Director of International Operations, ACTION. For a list of attendees, see APPENDIX B.
4:05–4:35	The President met with: Mr. Rumsfeld, Mr. Cheney
4:40–5:19	The President met with: Governor James E. Holshouser (R–North Carolina), Mr. Hartmann, Mr. Rumsfeld
5:20–5:25	The President met with: Congressman Richard Kelly (R–Florida), Lisa Lyon, 1974–75 Miss National Teenager, Mrs. E.G. Shaeffer, Miss National Teenager Pageant Director, Charles Leppert Jr., Special Assistant for Legislative Affairs
5:26–5:27	The President talked with Secretary Kissinger *[phone call received]*.
5:27–5:43	The President met with: William T. Coleman Jr., Secretary of Transportation, Mr. Cheney, William N. Walker, Director of the Presidential Personnel Office and Deputy Special Representative-designate for Trade Negotiations
5:47	The President went to the Cabinet Room.
5:47–7:12	The President attended a meeting to discuss the economy and energy. For a list of attendees, see APPENDIX C.
7:12	The President, accompanied by Vice President Nelson A. Rockefeller, returned to the Oval Office.

Telegrams

Telegrams are quick and easy primary sources to use with all ages of students. The messages are short and to the point with no punctuation. Telegrams give students ideas of what the world was like before e-mail. Telegrams are brief messages that students enjoy reading, interpreting, and comparing to modern-day communications. Tell students that the sender had to pay a block sum for the first 10 words and then had to pay additional money per letter after that. To save money, the messages were kept short.

The following is a telegram from Orville Wright to his father notifying him of the successful first flight at Kitty Hawk (Figure 4.1). Ask students to study the statement at the top about the Western Union Telegraph Company. Why do they think all this information is needed? Students can read the telegram and then decide where punctuation marks belong. Ask the students where the document was written and who received the document. Students should be able to identify what was important about this message and when it was written. These teaching strategies and questions can also easily be used with other telegrams.

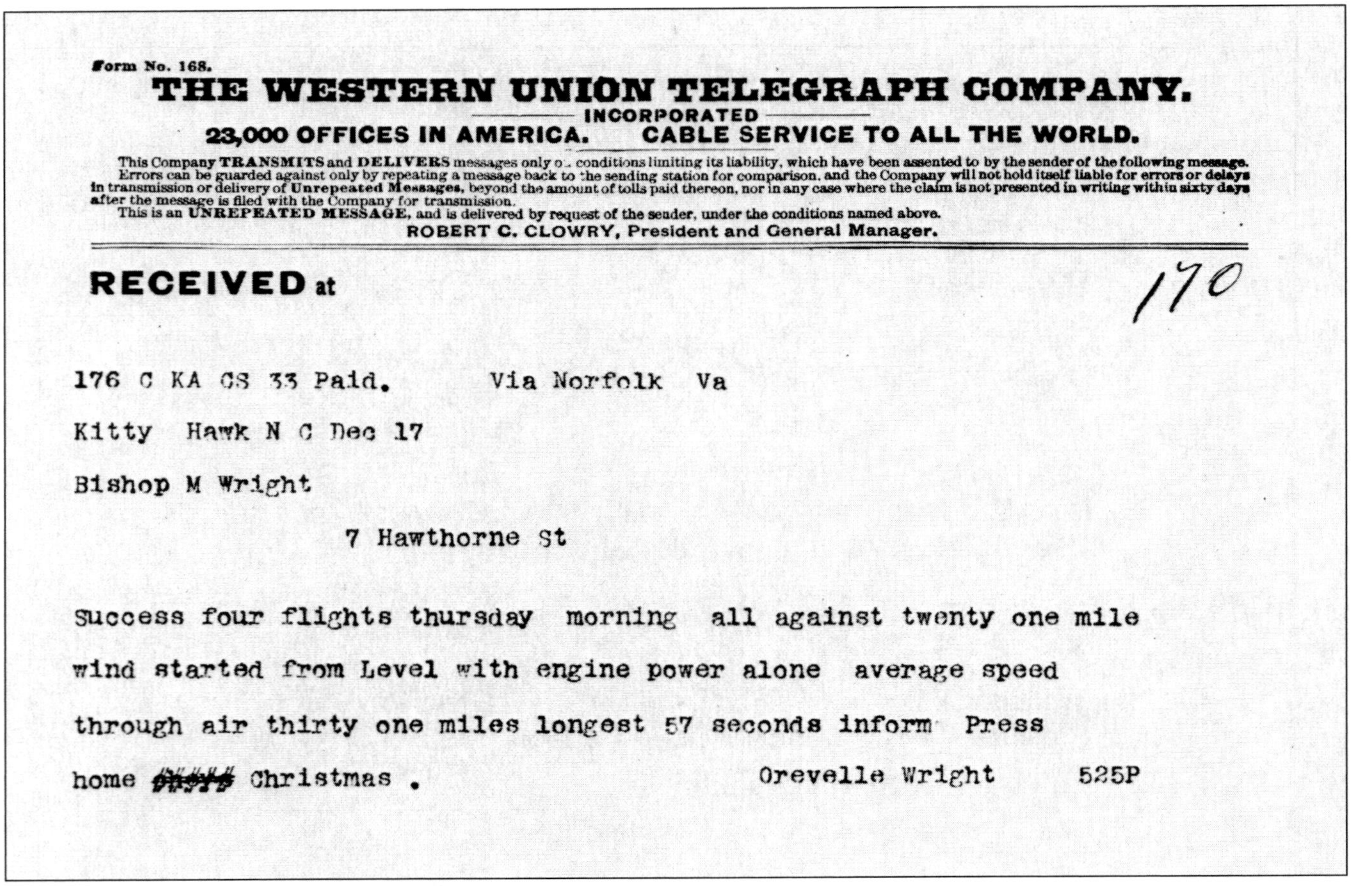

Form No. 168.

THE WESTERN UNION TELEGRAPH COMPANY.
INCORPORATED
23,000 OFFICES IN AMERICA.   CABLE SERVICE TO ALL THE WORLD.

This Company TRANSMITS and DELIVERS messages only o.. conditions limiting its liability, which have been assented to by the sender of the following message. Errors can be guarded against only by repeating a message back to the sending station for comparison, and the Company will not hold itself liable for errors or delays in transmission or delivery of Unrepeated Messages, beyond the amount of tolls paid thereon, nor in any case where the claim is not presented in writing within sixty days after the message is filed with the Company for transmission.
This is an UNREPEATED MESSAGE, and is delivered by request of the sender, under the conditions named above.
ROBERT C. CLOWRY, President and General Manager.

RECEIVED at   170

176 C KA GS 33 Paid.   Via Norfolk Va

Kitty Hawk N C Dec 17

Bishop M Wright

            7 Hawthorne St

Success four flights thursday morning all against twenty one mile

wind started from Level with engine power alone average speed

through air thirty one miles longest 57 seconds inform Press

home ~~flyis~~ Christmas .   Orevelle Wright   525P

Figure 4.1
Wright Brothers telegram
Source: The Library of Congress

Assignment: Design an assignment for students to write their own telegrams using the same format as the one above.

Letters

Letter writing is quickly becoming a lost art. The letters saved by families for generations have been keys to our social past. E-mails are helping families communicate across miles and to instantly share ideas, schedules, and experiences. Yet, this communication will, for the most part, never be archived nor read by future generations.

E-mails do not have the same flair as letters of the past did. There is little thought as to composition because e-mail is focused on making one's point and quickly sending the message to its destinations. However, it still is important for students to learn how to study and compose letters—especially ones that involve thanks.

Posing the following question might generate some interesting discussion: How will future generations learn about the social history of individuals in this generation if most of us rely on e-mail for communication?

Children's letters to a president are usually quite appropriate for elementary students. However, some subject matter contained in a letter is best studied at the middle school or high school level—which is the case with the letter to the right (Figure 4.2). This letter is from a young boy in Washington, D.C. The boy wrote to President John F. Kennedy following the church bombing in Birmingham, Alabama. With older students, you will have a much better discussion of the events surrounding this event and the reasons that President Kennedy did not send troops to Birmingham. Their own experiences may help them discuss the event and try to find solutions to the problems. Researching this famous bombing is intriguing to students.

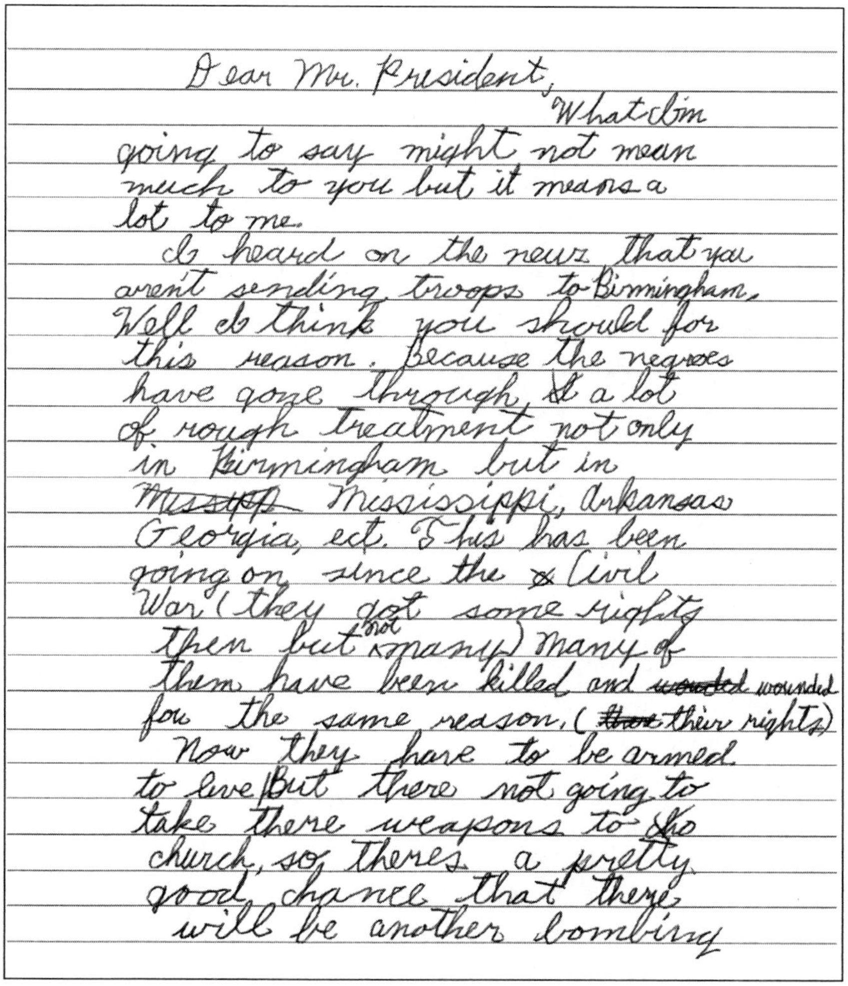

Dear Mr. President,

What I'm going to say might not mean much to you but it means a lot to me.

I heard on the news that you aren't sending troops to Birmingham. Well I think you should for this reason. Because the negroes have gone through a lot of rough treatment not only in Birmingham but in ~~Missipp~~ Mississippi, Arkansas Georgia, ect. This has been going on since the Civil War (they got some rights then but not many) Many of them have been killed and ~~wonded~~ wounded for the same reason, (~~that~~ their rights) Now they have to be armed to live. But there not going to take there weapons to the church, so there's a pretty good chance that there will be another bombing

Figure 4.2

Tom Oberdorfer's letter to President Kennedy

Source: The National Archives

Activity: Make a list of the kinds of questions students may have about this letter.

Drafts and Unpublished Sketches

First and second drafts of a literary work are especially interesting. But, they are often very difficult to find. By their very nature, first drafts are meant to be tossed away. Comparing a published piece with the drafts the author generated can give students insight into the thought process of an author. Students will also understand that even great authors have to revise and revise and revise. English teachers will welcome the opportunity to have examples of first drafts from published and respected authors.

The Library of Congress has first draft fragments of several of Walt Whitman's works: "Song of Myself" and "Leaves of Grass." They are easily accessed and show the changes he made as he wrote the poems. Figure 4.3 is a first draft of a stanza from "Song of Myself." What is your opinion of the changes Whitman made?

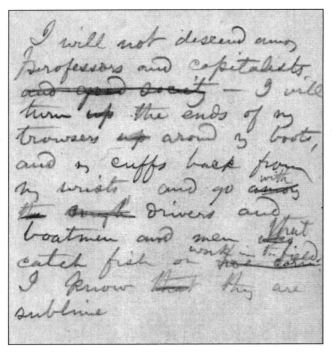

Figure 4.3

Page from Walt Whitman's first draft of "Song of Myself"
Source: The Library of Congress, Notebook LC #80

Scientific drafts of theories or research are also valuable primary sources that are difficult to obtain. Initial sketches of inventions are interesting resources and are available from the Library of Congress and museums that specialize in inventions. This is one of Alexander Graham Bell's sketches for a telephone (Figure 4.4), which looks similar to the can and string phones children construct at their own homes. Why do you think he scrapped this idea?

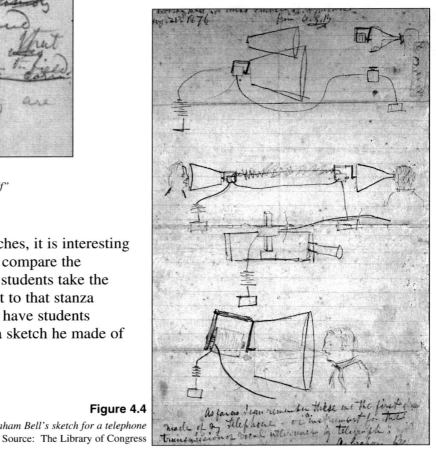

Figure 4.4

Alexander Graham Bell's sketch for a telephone
Source: The Library of Congress

For most drafts and unpublished sketches, it is interesting to students if they have the chance to compare the drafts to the final products. So, have students take the stanza from Figure 4.3 and compare it to that stanza in Whitman's "Song of Myself." Or, have students compare Bell's diagram sketch with a sketch he made of the final prototype of his invention.

Model Lessons and Activities

In the final pages of this chapter, four model lessons are provided for using unpublished and personal documents. The first two lessons are for grades 4–8, and the second two lessons are for grades 9–12. Each lesson provides a document and teaching strategies.

Unpublished Document Model Lesson 1 for Grades 4–8

To Governor George Clinton

Head Quarters, Valley Forge, February 16, 1778

Dear Sir:

It is with great reluctance, I trouble you on a subject, which does not fall within your province; but it is a subject that occasions me more distress, than I have felt, since the commencement of the war; and which loudly demands the most zealous exertions of every person of weight and authority, who is interested in the success of our affairs. I mean the present dreadful situation of the army for want of provisions, and the miserable prospects before us, with respect to futurity. It is more alarming than you will probably conceive, for, to form a just idea, it were necessary to be on the spot. For some days past, there has been little less, than a famine in camp. A part of the army has been a week, without any kind of flesh, and the rest for three or four days. Naked and starving as they are, we cannot enough admire the incomparable patience and fidelity of the soldiery, that they have not been ere this excited by their sufferings, to a general mutiny or dispersion. Strong symptoms, however, discontent have appeared in particular instances; and nothing but the most active efforts every where can long avert so shocking a catastrophe.

Our present sufferings are not all. There is no foundation laid for any adequate relief hereafter. All the magazines provided in the States of New Jersey, Pennsylvania, Delaware and Maryland, and all the immediate additional supplies they seem capable of affording, will not be sufficient to support the army more than a month longer, if so long. Very little has been done to the Eastward, and as little to the Southward; and whatever we have a right to expect from those quarters, must necessarily be very remote; and is indeed more precarious, than could be wished. When the forementioned supplies are exhausted, what a terrible crisis must ensue, unless all the energy of the Continent is exerted to provide a timely remedy!

George Washington

George Washington's letter to Governor Clinton, February 16, 1778

Model Lessons and Activities *(cont.)*

Unpublished Document Model Lesson 1 for Grades 4–8 *(cont.)*

Objectives

- Students will develop an understanding of the sacrifices and struggles that General Washington and his soldiers experienced at Valley Forge.

- Students will demonstrate their comprehension of the content of this document by completing a chart detailing the conditions at Valley Forge.

Teaching Strategies

1. Working in partners, students should analyze the document excerpt (page 79) to answer these questions: Who wrote this document? What is the document's date? What is the location? Who is to receive this document? What is the purpose of this document? What is the writer's point of view?

2. Then, tell the students the background of this document.

   General Washington is sitting out the winter at Valley Forge with starving soldiers and few provisions. He is frustrated and forced to beg for the supplies that he needs. His wife Martha joins him there, and she gathers other women to minister to the sick and dying. Governor George Clinton is serving as the first governor of New York. He was elected in 1777 after New York's constitutional convention and served until 1795. He was reelected again in 1801 and served until 1804. Washington is hoping that this governor will have the money and resources to help him get the needed provisions. Washington finally selects General Nathaniel Greene as the army quartermaster. He is able to deliver the needed supplies before the winter ends.

3. List the following words on an overhead and have students watch for these words as the document is real aloud: commencement, zealous exertions, provisions, incomparable, famine, fidelity, ere, dispersion, mutiny, magazines, precarious, and ensue. Use context clues and dictionaries as needed to help students understand their meanings.

4. Read the document together and have students paraphrase each sentence after it has been read.

5. Give the *Cause and Effect Document Analysis* (page 81) to pairs of students. This graphic organizer can be adjusted to fit any document. After students have completed the sheet, discuss in class what the students have written.

Extension Activity

Ask students to pretend they are soldiers at Valley Forge who are devoted followers of George Washington and the cause of freedom. They are to write letters from their points of view. The soldiers should write to their families to tell them about the conditions at the fort.

Model Lessons and Activities *(cont.)*

Unpublished Document Model Lesson 1 for Grades 4–8 *(cont.)*

Name_____

Cause and Effect Document Analysis

Directions: Using the text from the document, fill in the blanks for the cause-and-effect chart. Then, choose one research activity from the bottom of the page and complete it.

Cause	Effect
	Washington feels he must write to Governor Clinton for help.
	Soldiers are starving.
Starving soldiers are still patient and loyal.	
All the supplies provided by four states will not be sufficient.	
Supplies are completely exhausted.	

Research Activities

- Find out how General Nathaniel Green helped George Washington at Valley Forge.

- Find out how General von Steuben helped General Washington at Valley Forge.

- Find out how Martha Washington helped her husband at Valley Forge.

Model Lessons and Activities *(cont.)*

Unpublished Document Model Lesson 2 for Grades 4–8

From Leland Stanford to Abraham Lincoln
September 29, 1862

Time Received: 11 A.M.
Washington, D.C., October 1, 1862.

Sacramento Sept 29

As the Central Pacific RRd Co of California are desirous to commence the immediate prosecution of their portion of the Pacific RRd Will you please inform me what evidence you will require to fix the western base of Sierra Nevada Mountains as per section eleven of the Pacific Railroad Bill will the evidence of the United States Surveyor General of the state of California or either of them be sufficient

Please answer by telegraph

Leland Stanford
Gov of Cal

Telegraph message about the Pacific Railroad
Source: The Library of Congress

Model Lessons and Activities *(cont.)*

Unpublished Document Model Lesson 2 for Grades 4–8 *(cont.)*

Objectives

- Students will learn the format of a telegram and how it was the major source of cross-country communication in the 1800s.

- Students will write a telegram in a similar format to the one in this unit.

Teaching Strategies

1. Explain to students before they begin working with this document that telegrams do not have punctuation. Distribute photocopies of this telegram (page 82). Ask students to try to read it with a partner. Have pairs of students mark on their papers where they think punctuation belongs and what words need to be capitalized. Make sure they understand that RRD means railroad.

2. Put these words on the board or overhead and go over their meanings: desirous, commence, prosecution evidence, and sufficient. Students can write a synonym for each word above the words on their copies of the telegram.

3. Next, students will examine this telegram and answer basic questions about the document.

   - Who wrote this telegram?
   - Who received the telegram?
   - When was the telegram written?
   - What important events were happening at this time?
   - What is the purpose of this telegram?
   - Why does the sender need to know the answer to this question?

4. Meet back together as a class and read the document. Discuss what is being asked. Check on where students put punctuation. Have students report on their answers to the questions. Talk briefly about the Transcontinental Railroad.

5. Students will construct a telegram on a subject that suits your social-studies curriculum. The *Telegram Activity Sheet* (page 84) gives students specific directions on how to proceed. When students count the words, they only need to count the main paragraph and the closing line. It is a total of 74 words. The answers for the activity sheet are as follows:

   1. $22.90—$6.90 (first 10 words) + $16.00 (64 words x $.25) = $22.90

   2. $458.00 in today's money—$22.90 x 20 = $458

   3. Student telegrams will vary. Check students' math to make sure they figured out the costs correctly.

Model Lessons and Activities *(cont.)*

Unpublished Document Model Lesson 2 for Grades 4–8 *(cont.)*

Name: _____

Telegram Activity Sheet

Directions: Follow these steps to determine the cost of the Pacific Railroad message.

- Count all the words in the message except for the names, addresses, and dates. (That means you only count the main paragraph and the closing sentence.)

- In the 1860s, the first 10 words cost $2.45 if the telegram was sent to another place on the same coast. To go across the country, the first 10 words cost $6.90.

- Each additional word above 10 costs 25 cents.

- For example, a 20-word message from California to Washington, D.C., would cost— $6.90 (first 10 words) + $2.50 (10 more words) = $9.40.

- $1.00 in 1862 was about the same as $20.00 today. As a result, the $9.40 telegram in the example above would be worth $198.00 in today's money ($9.40 x 20).

1. How much would Stanford's Pacific Railroad message cost?

   _____

2. How much would the Pacific Railroad message be worth in today's money?

   _____

3. Pretend you live in 1862. Write a telegram about the railroad. Calculate how much it would cost to send your telegram from California to Washington, D.C., using the currency of 1862.

   _____

   _____

   _____

   _____

   _____

   _____

   _____

   _____

Model Lessons and Activities *(cont.)*

Unpublished Document Model Lesson 1 for Grades 9–12

. . . we've lost a lot of good men. It's only a question of time until we all get it. I'm all shot to pieces. I only hope I can stick it. I don't want to quit. My nerves are all gone and I can't stop. I've lived beyond my time already . . . . Here I am, twenty-four years old, I look forty and feel ninety. I've lost all interest in life beyond the next patrol. No one Hun will ever get me and I'll never fall into a trap, but sooner or later I'll be forced to fight against odds that are too long or perhaps a stray shot from the ground will be lucky and I will have gone in vain. Or my motor will cut out when we are trench strafing or a wing will pull off in a dive . . . . It gives me a dizzy feeling every time I hear of the men that are gone. And they have gone so fast I can't keep track of them; every time two pilots meet it is only to swap news of who's killed. When a person takes sick, lingers in bed a few days, dies and is buried on the third day, it all seems regular and they pass on into the great beyond in an orderly manner and you accept their departure as an accomplished fact. But when you lunch with a man, talk to him, see him go out and get in his plane in the prime of his youth and the next day someone tells you that he is dead—it just doesn't sink in and you can't believe it. And the oftener it happens the harder it is to believe. I've lost over a hundred friends, so they tell me . . . but to me they aren't dead yet. They are just around the corner, I think, and I'm still expecting to run into them any time. I dream about them at night when I do sleep a little.

Pilot's Diary Entry
Source: *War Birds Diary of an Unknown Aviator*

Background Information

In the early stages of World War I, pilots from the Allied and Axis forces flew in open cockpit bi-planes and tried to shoot each other down with pistols. Eventually, they used mounted machine guns and flew in squadrons. Very few of the young pilots lived to be called veterans, so their planes earned the name of "flying coffins." When the United States entered the war in 1917, American fighter patrols were stationed in France and flew over Germany. American pilots fought in major battles including St. Mihiel where 1,481 Allied planes fought in the skies. The leading U.S. flying aces included Edward Rickenbacker, 26 victories; Fredrick Gillet, 20 victories; and Wilfred Beaver, 19 victories.

Model Lessons and Activities *(cont.)*

Unpublished Document Model Lesson 1 for Grades 9–12 *(cont.)*

Objectives

- Students will learn about the early years of the army air corps and the extreme risks that World War I pilots took each day that they flew during that war.

- Students will analyze the emotions of a diary entry and summarize those feelings in a creative way.

Teaching Strategies

1. Distribute copies of the pilot's diary entry (page 85).

2. Read and discuss the background information with the class or use more detailed accounts that you have available. Explain that this diary entry is of an unknown pilot during World War I. What does that imply? Show a few images of WWI planes and discuss their open cockpits.

3. Have students work in pairs to read the pilot's diary entry and answer the following questions.

   - Was this written by an American or British pilot? Support your answer.

   - Did this pilot live or die during the war? Support your answer.

   - Divide the entry into three sections: exhaustion; facing death in an air battle; and loss of comrades. Tell which sentences fit each category. Which section is the longest? Does that surprise you? What does that tell you about the character of this young man?

   - What is the strongest part of this diary entry as to literary style?

   - What is the strongest part of this entry that gives information about flying in a battle during those times?

4. In pairs, have the students design creative ways to share the emotions that are portrayed in this diary entry. Examples include: write a poem; write a journal entry for the next day in his life using his style of writing; compare the feelings in this entry with a diary or letter from an American soldier in Iraq or other conflict (search Internet or other sources); research to find statistics about the number of pilots killed during WWI and what percentage of the air corps lost their lives; or write a memorial tribute to American military pilots.

Extension Activity

Research to find information about the lives of American WWI flying aces: Edward Rickenbacker, Fredrick Gillet, and Wilfred Beaver.

Model Lessons and Activities *(cont.)*

Unpublished Document Model Lesson 2 for Grades 9–12

This surprising message was handwritten by General Eisenhower in case the D-Day invasion failed.

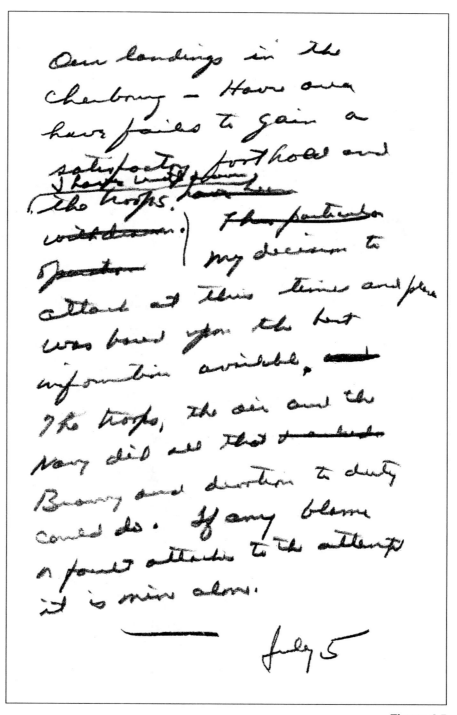

Figure 4.5
In Case of Failure Message from June 5, 1944
Source: Dwight D. Eisenhower Library

Model Lessons and Activities *(cont.)*

Unpublished Document Model Lesson 2 for Grades 9–12 *(cont.)*

Objectives

- Students will learn basic facts about the D-Day invasion as a major offensive battle in World War II.

- Students will analyze General Eisenhower's message and write an analysis of what this message reveals about Eisenhower's character and the importance of personal responsibility.

Teaching Strategies

1. Read some background information to the class regarding D-Day and include the role of General Eisenhower in this mission. Hold a class discussion about the significance of the event for the outcome of the war. Discuss what might have been the results if that mission had failed.

2. Pass out individual copies of the message written by General Eisenhower called *In Case of Failure* (Figure 4.5 on page 87). This document is also provided on the CD for your use (filename: dday.jpg).

3. Ask the students to read the message and write a two-sentence summary about what it means. Discuss as a class what they have written.

4. Discuss what it means to be responsible for one's actions and decisions. Ask students how this letter is an example of accepting responsibility. What does this letter show about the character of General Eisenhower?

5. Finally, have students write one-page essays on personal responsibility using General Eisenhower's character and this note as positive examples.

Extension Activity

Have students try to figure out what is strange about the date on this primary source.

Oral Histories and Interviews

Overview

Oral histories capture people's memories and experiences through sound recordings, videotapes, or written transcripts. Oral histories enable famous people, everyday citizens, and even those whose voices are frequently ignored to share their personal stories. Interviewing individuals about their memories of a certain time or event is an interactive process where the interviewer and the person being interviewed meet face to face and bond for a moment in time. Certain television reporters such as Barbara Walters are known for their fantastic interview skills.

Many historical societies have set a goal to record oral histories of their citizens who lived through certain eras or experiences. Each community wants to record the memories of citizens about the town's history; the experiences of immigrants; the stories about special events in the community long ago; stories from former students of the local high school to interpret how school experiences have changed over the years; explanations and video demonstrations from craftsmen and folk artists; tours given by people who have restored historic homes; or stories of everyday life during the Great Depression and other important eras.

Employees of presidential libraries spend their time conducting and collecting oral histories of people who knew the president during his early years as well as during his political career. The Library of Congress, the National Archives, and the Smithsonian Institution have special sections devoted to oral histories.

The Veterans History Project started by the Library of Congress has caught on in many communities and has been supported by civic organizations and school groups who have taken on the task of interviewing and recording these stories for future generations.

> *The goal of the Veterans History Project is to collect and preserve the firsthand accounts of U.S. veterans of all twentieth century wars from World War I to the Afghanistan and Iraq conflicts. In addition, those U.S. citizen civilians who were actively involved in supporting war efforts (such as war industry workers, USO workers, flight instructors, and medical volunteers) are also encouraged to contribute their personal narratives.*

The Library of Congress has a guide for conducting oral histories of veterans and the method for submitting them to their institution. The Smithsonian Institution also has an oral-history interviewing guide that can be accessed online.

Whether you choose to complete formal oral histories as a class project or less-formal interviews, students will gain confidence in themselves through the process. Planning the questions, setting up the interview time, and actually conducting the interview are all important interpersonal skills. Many students do not get opportunities to practice these skills in their everyday lives.

Class projects such as this also allow students the chance to touch base with people from older generations. Many times, young people do not have anything in common with their parents and grandparents. So, the lines of communication stay closed. These projects open up communication between family members and allow students the opportunities to look at life through the eyes of their ancestors.

Interview Skills

Each oral history interview is a personalized experience. While there are certain standard questions that all interviews include, much of what is asked by the interviewer should be based on meeting the goal of the interview. The interviewer must have enough focus to recognize good moments, to add a question to gain special insight, or to glean more depth from what the interviewee is sharing. Being able to think on the spot and ask the next question—even when the question is not on a list—is a skill that needs some practice. Student interviewers may feel shy when visiting with and listening to an adult about his or her experiences. The students may lack enough background to ask appropriate follow-up questions. Practicing interview skills in class will be helpful before students start any outside interview projects.

Prior to starting formal oral history projects, students should go through several steps. Students should begin by doing interviews in the class. Have students decide on topics of interest and prepare questions to pose to their fellow classmates. Then, have a day when students partner up and interview one another. This important first step allows quiet students a chance to practice their oral communication skills.

Next, assign short interview projects where students simply ask family members or neighbors a few questions on tape and then write reports of the answers to share with the class. These interviews should last two to five minutes.

The following are several topics that students can use to interview family members or neighbors who are 50 years or older. Students will probably have other ideas to add to this list:

- Share what you were doing on the day President Kennedy was assassinated. (Make a list of five questions about this topic.)

- Share what your high school experience was like. (Make a list of six questions about this topic.)

- Share how it felt to grow up in the fifties and sixties.

- What did you do on Sundays when you were growing up?

Questions for people who are 30 years and older:

- What do you remember about the day the *Challenger* exploded on takeoff?

- What organizations, jobs, and activities did you participate in while in high school? What did you gain from those experiences?

- What were your favorite toys when you were in elementary school? Why did you like them?

- How did you play with those toys—by yourself, with friends, or with siblings?

Finally, you can have a parent day in your classroom. Invite parents of your students in to class to be interviewed. Have your students interview the parents of their peers. Asking parents for brief biographies ahead of time will allow students enough information to prepare interview questions. After one or more of these more casual steps, your students should be ready to participate in a more formal interview or oral history project.

Class Interview Project

When planning a class interview project, you might want to follow these steps.

- **Decide on a group of people to interview.** Students can interview people who worked on the home front during World War II; people who emigrated to your community from another country; people who have adopted children from overseas; people who started a community project; or many others.

- **Establish a reason to interview specific people.** Students may want to know what work was like during World War II and how people on the home front needed to make sacrifices. Students may want to know the most difficult and most rewarding experiences people went through in their emigration from their homelands to your community. Students may want to learn why people want to adopt children from foreign countries and what those parents have learned that might help others who are interested in adopting children from other countries. Students may want to understand why people started a community project and why it becomes successful.

- **Decide what students will do with these interviews once they are completed.** Will the recordings be given to your local archives? Will they be edited and used in a production? Will the interviews be shown as a continuous video at a special event where the people who were interviewed will be honored? Or, will students make written transcripts and edit the interviews and publish these in a book format?

- **Generate a list of people to interview and access their addresses and phone numbers.** Then, contact the people you want to interview to set up appointments. Set up a place to conduct the interview where there will be little chance for outside noise or interruptions. Ask someone to help run the interview equipment such as video recorder or tape recorder.

- **Research the topic, group, or time period pertaining to the upcoming interview.** This is the piece students usually want to skip, but it is really critical. Reporters call it, "Doing your homework." Students need to read, ask questions, and research in the library and on the Internet to get some background information on the topic of the interview. This research will lead them to ask more appropriate and more productive questions.

- **Brainstorm some important questions to cover in the interview.**

- **Watch some taped interviews to see the techniques of the reporters.** How did the reporters get the interviewees to relax and be able to chat rather than to quote a few memorized lines? What kind of questions did the reporters ask? What kind of follow-up questions did the reporters add that had not been planned?

- **Revise and refine questions.**

- **Double-check the equipment and room reservations.**

- **Call the interviewees to confirm appointment times.**

- **Conduct the interviews at the scheduled times and places.**

Model Lesson and Activity

Analyzing Oral Histories Model Lesson for Grades 9–12

Objectives

- Students will learn about a historical event from a firsthand account.

- Students will analyze an oral history interview and write down information about its components. They will pay attention to the quality of the skills the interviewer uses and learn techniques for conducting their own interviews.

Teaching Strategies

1. Select an oral-history transcript or an audio or video oral history from your local county archives or one of the many listed on the Internet. The American Folk Life Center at the Library of Congress is a good online resource. The interviews of Pearl Harbor eyewitnesses and survivors are available, for example. The Center for Oral History at the University of Hawaii at Manoa preserves the recollections of Hawaii's people through oral interviews and disseminates oral-history transcripts to researchers, students, and the general community. (See pages 171–172 for more information on these online resources.)

2. Give students copies of the *Oral History Questions* (pages 94–95). Review the questions with the students prior to reading the transcript or listening to the audio or video recording.

3. Read the transcript or play the audio or video recording. Have students write their responses to the questions. If you read a transcript of an oral history, treat it like a reader's theater script by having one student read the interviewer part and another read the responses of the person being interviewed.

4. Discuss the quality of the interview and what information was gained. Why is it important for everyday people to have a chance to be heard? Are they also a part of history?

Model Lesson and Activity *(cont.)*

Analyzing Oral Histories Model Lesson for Grades 9–12 *(cont.)*

- -

Name_____

Oral History Questions

1. Who was interviewed?

_____

2. Who conducted the interview?

_____

3. What was the purpose of the interview?

_____

_____

4. How long was the interview?

_____

5. Was this enough time to get the information needed?

_____

6. Did the interviewer stick to a list of questions or did he/she use follow-up questions that referred back to what the interviewee had just said? Or both?

_____

_____

7. Did the interviewer get some basic facts about the interviewee's life at the beginning of the interview? What kind of information?

_____

_____

_____

Model Lesson and Activity *(cont.)*

Analyzing Oral Histories Model Lesson for Grades 9–12 *(cont.)*

Oral History Questions *(cont.)*

8. How did the interviewer make the person being interviewed feel at ease?

_____

_____

_____

9. Summarize the main points of the interview.

_____

_____

_____

_____

_____

_____

10. What especially interesting tidbits did you get from hearing/viewing this interview?

_____

_____

_____

_____

_____

11. What lessons did you gain from listening to this interview regarding interviewing skills and techniques?

_____

_____

_____

_____

_____

Notes

Political Cartoons and Comic Strips

Overview

This chapter discusses the role of comics and cartoons in culture and how studying cartoons gives insight into our past social structure. A brief history of political or editorial cartoons will also be explored through examples. General questions and activities for cartoons are provided throughout.

From the beginning, political and editorial cartoons were designed to send a message, to make a point, to influence opinion, or to ridicule. By their very nature, they have obvious points of view. The history of political cartoons on American soil started during colonial times with Benjamin Franklin who occasionally inserted caricatures and cartoons in his newspaper. At that time, cartoons were very difficult to reproduce for printing, so they did not appear on a regular basis in newspapers. Reproducing cartoons involved the laborious and time-consuming process of cutting wood blocks for engraving. The famous political cartoon (Figure 6.1) called "Join or Die" is one of the earliest examples of political persuasion in the colonies. At that time, there was a superstition that a snake cut apart could rejoin itself. The cartoon was published by Benjamin Franklin in the Pennsylvania Gazette on May 9, 1754, to convince the colonies to stick together and fight with Great Britain against the French in the French and Indian War. Many people today look at the cartoon and assume it was designed to encourage colonies to join together during the Revolutionary War—which is not the case. This cartoon is often found on state and national tests. Students can analyze this to determine what the letters on the snake parts mean. They can also discuss the missing colony of Georgia. Why was that colony left off the snake?

Figure 6.1
"Join or Die"
Source: The Woods Publishing Company

Assignment: Write a document-based question about this cartoon.

Overview *(cont.)*

Another political cartoon from the late 1700s appeared in *The Centinel* on January 30, 1788 (Figure 6.2). The cartoon was called "The Federal Pillars" and showed a divine hand raising the Massachusetts column to an upright position. *The Centinel* newspaper supported the new Constitution and was pushing for ratification. Some pillars are shown in an upright position since they had already ratified the Constitution. Which states were these? What is the point of view of the artist?

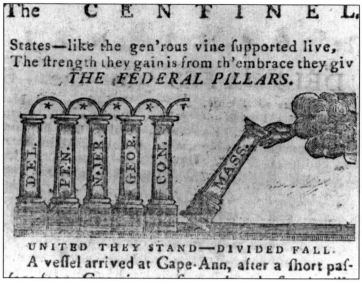

Figure 6.2
"The Federal Pillars"
Source: The Library of Congress

Political cartooning and caricatures gained popularity in England in the 1780s, when James Gillray produced lithographs ridiculing the British royalty. In 1841, a British comic weekly called *Punch* hit the newsstands. It used wit and satire to criticize and expose celebrities, royalty, and politicians. *Punch* featured cartooning and caricatures that set the stage for the "political cartoon" as we know it today. Political cartoons featured in *Punch* influenced government leaders and public opinion until 1992 when it ceased publication. Students can compare front covers of *Punch* issues from different generations and list the hot political topics of each era.

During the Civil War, political engravings were popular types of political cartoons. This political engraving, the "Fugitive Slave Act" (Figure 6.3), shows Northern abolitionists on the left side, including William Lloyd Garrison, protecting a slave woman, and the supporters of the enforcement of the Fugitive Slave Act, including Secretary of State Daniel Webster, on the right side. Riding Webster's back is a portly slave catcher swinging a noose and manacles. Using a magnifying glass or hand lens, one can read that the two flags flying from the Temple of Liberty have specific statements about the evils of this act. Students examining this type of cartoon should describe the action on each side and then compare and contrast the two sides. What kind of violence is being portrayed on each side? What is the artist's point of view?

Figure 6.3
"Fugitive Slave Act"
Source: The Library of Congress

Assignment: Write three questions about one of the two cartoons on this page. Write questions for these three levels of Bloom's Taxonomy: comprehension, application, and analysis.

Overview *(cont.)*

President Abraham Lincoln was a popular topic for political engravings, especially during the first presidential campaign against Stephen Douglas. To correctly analyze this cartoon (Figure 6.4), called the "Presidential Footrace," students would need to notice the statures of the two main characters and the fact that a slave is watching the race. Students should be able to recognize that Lincoln was tall and lanky and Douglas was short and stout. How might this give Lincoln the advantage in a race. Conducting a discussion about comparing a foot race to a presidential race will help students grasp the analogy.

Other symbols that need to be understood in order to appreciate or interpret the cartoon are the rail fence and the capitol building. The comments of each character show their backgrounds—Lincoln can easily go over the fence, since he built the fence. Douglas is behind in the race and is being criticized by the slave. By today's standards, the cartoon might be considered offensive due to the submissive language of the slave. It is important to note that cartoons reflect the time in which they were drawn and the prejudices that were prevalent in those times.

Figure 6.4
"Presidential Footrace"
Source: The Library of Congress

Assignment: Discuss with another teacher whether you would want to use this cartoon in your classroom. What are the possible problems with using this cartoon in your classroom? What are some reasons for using this cartoon? What grade level should study this cartoon? What are some effective strategies to use with this cartoon? These are the types of questions to ask about some primary sources before you decide to use them—not after a problem has risen.

Overview *(cont.)*

Throughout the 1800s, political cartoons were found in weekly and monthly magazines, such as *Harper's Weekly*. Thomas Nast was one of *Harper's Weekly*'s most popular cartoonists. His most famous political cartoon campaign focused on ousting the Boss Tweed Ring (Figure 6.5). What is Nast saying about Tweed in this cartoon? How can this story of a brave artist's crusade against crime be used in your classroom?

Figure 6.5

"Stone Walls Do Not a Prison Make" by Thomas Nast
Source: The Library of Congress

Tweed was furious about Nast's cartoons and yelled, "Stop them damned pictures. I don't care what the papers write about me. My constituents can't read. But, they can see pictures." Tweed offered Nast one-half million dollars to leave the United States and move to Europe, which Nast promptly rejected. The attempted bribe increased Nast's desire to see Tweed behind prison bars. When Tweed fled the United States for Spain, Nast produced another cartoon picture of Tweed—which was read by Spanish authorities who were then able to find Tweed and arrest him. Why did the Spanish police think that Tweed was wanted for kidnapping when they viewed the magazine cover below (Figure 6.6)?

Figure 6.6

"Tweed-le-dee and Tilden-dum" by Thomas Nast
Source: The Library of Congress

Thomas Nast also created the Republican Party's elephant and made the Democratic Party's donkey a popular symbol. When Americans think of Santa Claus, they are remembering Nast's 1860s drawing of a jolly Santa with a round belly, a red nose, and a pipe in his hand. Perhaps Nast got his idea for his drawing from Clement C. Moore's poem, "A Visit from St. Nicholas"—popularly known today as "'Twas the Night Before Christmas."

Overview *(cont.)*

When technology allowed higher-quality images in newspapers, cartooning really took off and became part of daily newspapers such as James Pulitzer's *New York World* and William Randolph Hearst's *New York Evening Journal*. The courting of creative cartoonists to work at each newspaper was part of the legendary battles of yellow journalism. Without the modern telecommunication network we have today, the daily newspaper was the citizen's link to local, national, and world news. Those who could read, devoured the paper from front to back, and political cartoons were an entertaining component.

John Keppler and Carl Schurz, both of German ancestry, were two popular political cartoonists of the Gilded Age. Keppler published the first commercially illustrated humor magazine popular in America and by 1880, that magazine, *Puck*, claimed a circulation of 85,000 readers. The cartoons featured in *Puck* showed a liberal orientation and advocated social reform.

The styles that dominated during the 1880s and the prevailing years set the stage for modern political cartoons. Many of the symbols we recognize in today's cartoons came from that era. What symbols in Figure 6.7 are familiar? What wording or abbreviations are used? Who are the two main characters? What does the bridge represent? How do you know? What does the ball and chain mean? In order for students to successfully answer these questions, they must learn about symbolism and structure in political cartoons.

Figure 6.7
"I Think I'll Walk"
Source: The Library of Congress

Another famous cartoonist, Clifford Berryman (1896–1949), created the Teddy Bear, which appeared in one of his cartoons (Figure 6.8) after President Theodore Roosevelt refused to kill a bear cub that had wandered into his campsite during a hunting trip. How has the symbol become an icon of our culture?

Students can look at political cartoons from 100 years ago and learn the history of icons they're familiar with today. Students will enjoy comparing and contrasting symbols from then and now.

Figure 6.8
"To Go or Not to Go" by Clifford Berryman
Source: The National Archives

Finding Political Cartoons

The job of finding political cartoons for classroom use is much easier today than it has been in the past. Educators can make a copy of a cartoon to display in class or can reproduce cartoons in small quantities for students without obtaining copyright permission.

Your local newspaper will have numerous examples of political cartoons that are appropriate for your classroom, depending on the age of your students. Your judgment will be critical in making selections that fit your curriculum and your student audience. Since political cartoons reflect current events, they are terrific teaching tools about public opinion. The symbols and caricatures in modern cartoons may need some explanation for students who are not familiar with current events and who do not know who's who in the world scene. Using some recent political cartoons as examples when studying about symbols is a useful exercise. The Library of Congress, the National Archives, the presidential libraries and museums, and other online sources have historic cartoon collections that you can find using Internet search engines.

When selecting a cartoon for study, it is important to ask: What would students need to know or find out in order to understand this cartoon? Does the cartoon suit the issue we are studying or does it require too much explanation to be worth studying at this time? Should a brief background history of the cartoon be given to students before or after studying the cartoon?

In Figure 6.9, shown below, what do students need to know in order to understand the message of the cartoon? The names of the men are not evident. Can students without a good background in New York history understand the point of the cartoon? Questions like these can help you decide which political cartoons are most appropriate for your classroom.

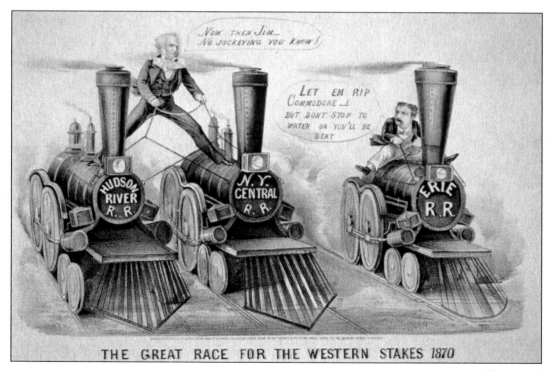

Figure 6.9
"The Great Race for the Western Stakes"
Source: The Library of Congress

Teaching with Political Cartoons

For the most part, political cartoons are best suited for middle school and high school classrooms. The understanding of satire, symbolism, analogies, and current or historical events are prerequisites for interpreting political cartoons in depth. For example, Figure 6.10 holds little meaning without students knowing who the two caricatures represent or what event is being referenced.

Political cartoons should be examined on several levels so that students can learn in stages how to study these artistic political statements. Almost all cartoons have similar elements and they are listed below. Instruct and show students how to identify these elements and how to recognize a variety of common symbols.

Figure 6.10

"Play Bluff"
Source: The Woods Publishing Group

- Each political cartoon has a title and sometimes a caption that give a clue about the cartoon's meaning.

- Each political cartoon has objects or people that participate in some action.

- Each political cartoon uses symbols that the artist assumes the audience will understand. (e.g., donkey, elephant, Uncle Sam, hammer and sickle, American flag, Union Jack, Big Ben, the capitol dome, the White House, the Statue of Liberty, ball and chain)

- Some political cartoons have characters who make comments in the cartoon.

- Some characters or objects in political cartoons have labels that help the reader understand the message.

- Each political cartoon uses persuasion, so there is an overall message to convey and the cartoonist always has a point of view.

- Each political cartoon is best understood by the people of the time period when the cartoon was created. What was timely, funny, or satirical then may have less meaning today.

- People in the political cartoon may be caricatures with exaggerated features. Why are those features exaggerated?

- Political cartoons frequently use analogies to get points across.

- Irony or satire may be obvious or subtle in political cartoons.

Types of Questions to Use with Cartoons

Once students learn the main elements of political cartoons, they are ready to respond to questions. Below are three levels of questions that can be used with different grade levels to interpret the many layers of meaning in a cartoon. For example, fourth graders can answer the basic-level questions; eighth graders can answer questions from both the basic and intermediate levels; while high school students should be able to answer questions from all levels.

Basic Level

- What is the cartoon's caption or title?

- Identify the people and objects in the cartoon.

- What words or phrases are used in the cartoon?

- Who is the cartoonist?

Intermediate Level

- What symbols are used in this cartoon? What does each symbol mean?

- What are the most important words or phrases in this cartoon? Why are they important?

- Did the artist exaggerate any physical features of the people in the cartoon? Explain those exaggerations.

- What is difficult to understand about this cartoon? Explain.

- What is the main point of this cartoon? How did the artist use persuasive techniques?

- What is the analogy in this cartoon? What two issues, ideas, objects, or situations are being compared?

Advanced Level

- What groups would agree with this cartoon? What groups would disagree? Explain your answers.

- What background information must one understand in order to interpret this cartoon?

- What do you know about the artist's political views from studying this cartoon?

- How is irony or satire used in this cartoon?

Political Cartoons and Parts of Speech

A political cartoon is a picture sentence conveying a point of view. One way for students to analyze a political cartoon and at the same time cover the basic parts of speech is to view a cartoon and determine its subject, verb, and object. Once this has been accomplished, students write a complete sentence conveying the cartoon's theme or message. More than one-sentence interpretations can be made using any cartoon as the springboard.

Show Figure 6.11 to students and help them analyze the two characters. Which could be the subject? What could be an action verb in each case? Actually, either character or both characters could be the subject—depending on how the student wants to word the sentence. Here are two possible examples:
1) Congress wants to use the FBI for their purposes, but Truman says, "No."
2) Truman insists that Congress not interfere in the executive branch and stay on their side of the fence.

In the cartoon below (Figure 6.12), a more complex sentence is needed. "The Democratic Donkey digs up issues while the Republican Elephant digs the Panama Canal," is one possible option.

Figure 6.11

"Hope this won't develop into a neighborhood feud"
Source: The National Archives

Figure 6.12

"A Real Chore"
Source: The National Archives

Assignment: Write three other sentence options for the Truman cartoon above (Figure 6.11). Discuss the analogy of this cartoon. What information would students need to understand this cartoon? Why is the fence an important symbol that explains the cartoon's message?

Strip and Single Frame Comics

Comics can be single-frame comics such as *Family Circus* and *The Far Side*. They can also be multi-frame comic strips found in daily newspapers or in comic books. Over the generations, readers have called these types of cartoons by various names: comics, the funnies, and strips. Comic strips appearing in newspapers have familiar characters that people associate with the series. Examples are *Peanuts*, *Blondie*, and *Dennis the Menace*. Some strips such as *Mark Trail* and *Brenda Starr* have been featured for generations. At one time, Sunday comics were very popular, had large followings, and were even a topic of discussion at work. In the *Dick Tracy* comic, Li'l Abner and Daisy Mae getting married and Sparkle Plenty being born were big events and major topics of conversation.

Comic books were a popular reading distraction prior to television and are now highly collectible. Occasionally, biographical comic books were designed to highlight a famous person's life. The Democratic Party used the Truman comic book (Figure 6.13) as propaganda during the 1948 campaign to help the voting public understand why Truman was qualified to be elected president. This is page four of the booklet. What qualities of Truman's life does this page depict?

Figure 6.13

Truman comic book
Source: Truman Presidential Museum and Library

Strip and Single Frame Comics *(cont.)*

One popular comic series that later became the basis of a Broadway musical was *Little Orphan Annie*. In these two carton strips (Figures 6.14 and 6.15), Daddy Warbucks is frustrated about losing his fortune during the Great Depression. The cartoons address the main economic and social issue of the time. How could these comic strips be used during the study of the Great Depression? Are these types of propaganda? What do these comic strips say about the artist's views of the Depression?

Figure 6.14

Little Orphan Annie "Shucks! Is That All?"
Source: Tribune Media Services, Inc.

In Figure 6.15, a millionaire is forced to hunt for a job and lacks qualifications for the jobs available, which was a common occurrence during the Depression. What did Warbucks always believe prior to his current situation? What does he believe now?

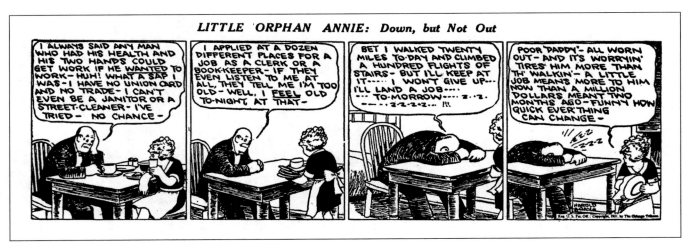

Figure 6.15

Little Orphan Annie "Down, but Not Out"
Source: Tribune Media Services, Inc.

Assignment: Students can compare and contrast the moods in these two comic strips. Write a follow-up activity for these two comic strips.

Strip and Single Frame Comics *(cont.)*

The *Brenda Starr* comic strip began in 1940 and was the only strip at that time created by a woman. It is still published today under the artistic work of another female artist. Comparing old comic strips, such as *Brenda Starr*, with the same comic from today is a useful compare-and-contrast activity for students. Students enjoy comparing fashions Brenda wore in 1940 to today and the job assignments she had. Check with your local newspaper's archives for a copy of one of the older strips. She sure looks good for her age and for working over 60 years at the same job, too!

Comic books are still produced today, but are mostly focused on action series. Comparing an old Batman comic book with a modern-day Batman book is an interesting activity to hone students' observation skills. Batman originated in 1939 and is unique because he has no super powers, and he relies on his intellect. Check with a flea market to see if one of the comic-book vendors might share some old comics with your students. What can one determine about the culture of the times in which a cartoon or comic is created?

For your information, collectors of comic books have divided the publications into eras:

The Platinum Age: 1897–1932

The Golden Age: 1933–1945

The Atomic Age: 1946–August 1956

The Silver Age: September 1956–1969

The Bronze Age: 1970–1979

The Modern Age: 1980—Present

Additional Ideas

Here are three additional ideas for using comic books in the classroom.

- Give students a comic and ask them to attempt to label the comic by its era, based on cultural clues such as the clothing and setting.
- For each comic strip, students can name the characters, the setting, the plot, and the cultural icons and images featured.
- Students can design a comic strip about a current or historic event or about a school issue.

Model Lessons and Activities

On the next few pages, you will find three model lessons using political cartoons. Each lesson provides objectives, strategies, and activities. Enjoy using cartoons in your classroom and teaching your students the tools and strategies for interpreting these images.

Political Cartoon Model Lesson for Grades 4–8

Figure 6.16
"Election Day!"
Source: The Library of Congress

Model Lessons and Activities *(cont.)*

Political Cartoon Model Lesson for Grades 4–8 *(cont.)*

Objectives

- Students will learn basic facts about the struggle for women to gain the right to vote.

- Students will analyze the political cartoon by answering questions about the artist's focus. They will compare and contrast this cartoon scene to one that might be drawn today showing family members leaving to vote at the polls.

Teaching Strategies

1. Provide each student with a copy of the "Election Day!" cartoon (Figure 6.16) or make a transparency and show this cartoon on the overhead. This political cartoon is also provided on the CD for your use (filename: voting.jpg).

2. Have students answer and discuss the following questions.

   - Describe the setting of this cartoon. Where do the characters live—city, farm, or suburb? Explain your answer.

   - The cartoon was drawn in 1909. How is life different today from life in 1909? Explain your answer.

   - Who are the main characters? Describe how they are dressed.

   - What is the woman going to do? Why is this so unusual? What does the man think about the situation?

   - What do you think the setting will be like when the woman returns?

   - When did women receive the right to vote through an amendment to the United States Constitution? Was it before or after the date of this cartoon? Why can this woman vote at this time?

   - In what ways do we really appreciate the right to vote and the sacrifices others made to give us that right?

Extension Activity

Describe a home scene today in which parents are leaving to go vote. How is your scene different from the one depicted in 1909? Draw a cartoon titled "Modern Election Day!" that shows a modern version of the same topic.

Model Lessons and Activities *(cont.)*

Political Cartoon Model Lesson 1 for Grades 9–12

Figure 6.17

"The Macmillion"

Source: The Library of Congress

Background Information

This cartoon of Andrew Carnegie (1835–1919) as the "Macmillion" appeared in *Punch* magazine in 1901 and shows Carnegie dressed in a kilt. Carnegie was a Scottish immigrant to the United States who made his fortune in the steel industry. Carnegie sold his company in 1900 to J.P. Morgan for $480 million and began a new adventure of giving away his money. Part of his money went to Scottish charities and universities. Carnegie was one of the greatest philanthropists of all time, creating a network of public libraries and music halls in the United States.

Model Lessons and Activities *(cont.)*

Political Cartoon Model Lesson 1 for Grades 9–12 *(cont.)*

Objectives

- Students will make plans for donating Carnegie's money and describe his role in promoting positive results in our society.

- Students will analyze a political cartoon answering questions about the focus the artist intended.

Teaching Strategies

1. Either make a transparency of "The Macmillion" (Figure 6.17) or photocopy the cartoon for groups to use. This political cartoon is also provided on the CD for your use (filename: carnegie.jpg).

2. Then, have students read the background information and study the cartoon. Students will answer the following questions about the cartoon.

   - Why was the cartoon called "The Macmillion" rather than something connected to Carnegie's name?

   - Why would Carnegie's kilt be made from an American flag?

   - What does the bag hanging from his waist symbolize?

   - What were the four Scottish universities to which Carnegie donated money according to the cartoon?

   - What is the main point of this cartoon?

   - Is the artist trying to persuade, inform, or entertain the reader? Explain your answer.

   - Why would Carnegie donate so much money to Scotland?

   - What question would you like to ask the artist? What question would you like to ask Andrew Carnegie?

   - What background information must one understand in order to interpret this cartoon?

   - Research one of the institutions that benefited from Carnegie's money. What is that institution doing today?

3. Tell students that they have been placed in charge of Carnegie's money. Explain that he wants them to produce a list of ideas about where he can donate his money for good causes. The students should each come up with at least five causes on which Carnegie can spend his money. For each idea, students should include their reasons for their choice. Then, they should draw a new political cartoon showing Carnegie giving his money to one or two of their causes. When students are finished, have them share their cartoons and/or display them in your room.

Model Lessons and Activities *(cont.)*

Political Cartoon Model Lesson 2 Grades 9–12 *(cont.)*

Figure 6.18
"Life on the Mississippi"
Source: The National Archives

Model Lessons and Activities *(cont.)*

Political Cartoon Model Lesson 2 Grades 9–12 *(cont.)*

Objectives

- Students will discuss the role of a president in working with the legislature on getting bills passed and in working toward reform.

- Students will analyze this political cartoon answering questions about the analogy the artist intended.

Teaching Strategies

1. Make photocopies of this cartoon (Figure 6.18) for student partners to study. This political cartoon is also provided on the CD for your use (filename: missrvr.jpg). The cartoon should be used in conjunction with the study of the presidency of Theodore Roosevelt, the study of trusts and antitrust legislation, or the study of the role of a president within the three branches of government.

2. Then, have students complete the following activities:

   - Describe all the symbols and images you see in this cartoon. What is happening in the cartoon? Is the river also a type of symbol? Explain.

   - What analogy is being used to convey the artist's point? What background information do you need to catch the analogy? What other famous person is Roosevelt being compared to in this cartoon? Does the cartoon's real meaning have anything to do with the Mississippi River? Why or why not?

   - Write a one-sentence summary of this cartoon using some form of the verb "navigate."

   - What issues are being mentioned in this cartoon? Quickly research in your text or another resource and find information on each issue. Write a two-sentence description of each trust or interest group that is mentioned.

   - Read in your history text to find out how successful Roosevelt was in dealing with trusts and interest groups.

Extension Activity

What issues are facing the current president? Design a cartoon using another navigation (land, air, sea, river) analogy to show how the current president is confronting those issues.

General Analysis Strategies

These strategies can be used with any political cartoon or comic strip. Students can:

- Draw a cartoon using the same characters but portraying the opposite point of view.

- Add a few "sentence bubbles" with comments made by the characters.

- Write a letter either agreeing or disagreeing with the cartoon's point of view. The letter should be written to the editor of the newspaper that printed this cartoon.

- Write a different title for the cartoon and explain why they chose their new title.

- Write a short background history for the cartoon explaining the events that led up to the event shown in the cartoon.

- Compare and contrast several cartoons from different artists about the same subject. They will make a list of similarities and differences and explain which artist did the best job getting his point across.

- Imagine how difficult it would be to create a cartoon on a daily basis that shows a special political point of view. They can write a letter to a cartoonist asking how it is possible to maintain creativity on a regular schedule.

- Compare cartoons from several newspapers of the same date to determine what social or political issue gained the most attention on that date. Do any of the newspapers use the same cartoonist? Do different cartoonists have different or similar points of view about the issue?

- Draw a cartoon about a school issue for their school newspaper.

Maps

Overview

Studying modern maps gives students a sense of where they are in the world and a perspective of the vast resources, the different cultures, and the political boundaries that make up their region, country, and world. Studying maps from the past provides students with an understanding of how people once described their environments and how cartography has changed over the centuries.

This chapter discusses the role maps have played in human culture and how humans have perceived their world over time. A brief history of cartography will also be explored through examples. A variety of map styles will be demonstrated, and general questions and activities for interpreting primary source maps will be provided.

Before and during the study of primary source maps, some basic skills and background knowledge is needed for students to understand how maps are interpreted. These skills are taught from the early grades through high school. Students should:

- survey different types of maps as illustrated in this chapter.

- study and interpret the different parts of maps such as scale of miles; compass rose; symbols for features such as boundaries, rivers, mountains, and cities; legends; and the grid system associated with longitude and latitude.

- prepare a scale of miles or kilometers that mimics the scale on a map and use that scale to measure map distances.

- learn geographical terms such as island, peninsula, estuary, bay, prime meridian, meridian, longitude, latitude, equator, knots, leagues, perspective, and projection.

- develop a basic understanding of the history of cartography and the role exploration, governmental changes, and scientific data have played in the evolution of maps over the years.

- understand that maps are designed in a variety of styles for a variety of purposes.

Use the following general questions when studying maps:

- What type of map is this?
- What is the title of the map?
- What is the date of the map?
- Who is the mapmaker (cartographer)?
- Why was the map created?
- What are the map's main features?
- Are there any inscriptions on the map or written descriptions?
- Where was it produced?
- What is the scale of the map?
- Is there a legend? Describe the legend.
- Are there any artistic features on the map? Describe them in detail.
- Is this map still accurate today? Why or why not?
- Who would use this map?
- How does this map relate to the topic you are studying?

Styles of Maps

Maps are used on a daily basis by aviators, truck drivers, tourists, real-estate agents, city officials, contractors, weather forecasters, news teams, and military leaders. Average citizens can simply conduct an Internet search to locate a detailed map and directions to help them get to their destinations. However, historians also study maps to gain information about how previous generations viewed their world. Military maps tell stories of how armies of the past planned their strategies. Early explorers drew maps based on walking or sailing through an area. Studying map renditions helps us appreciate the talents of people who created maps with so little information and with only the most basic surveying tools.

Old maps reveal what changes have occurred in different regions. What is today a shopping mall was at one time a series of farms. What was once a territory is now divided into several states. This map of Spanish territory (Figure 7.1) shows California as an island. What would have made the mapmaker believe that it was an island? How can you tell that the cartographer was Spanish?

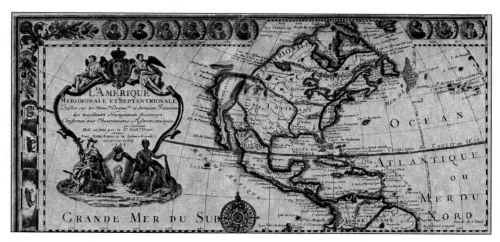

Figure 7.1

Old map of California
Source: Historical Documents, Co.

Experts frequently use the perspective of maps for classification. A perspective view and bird's-eye view are different names for a **panoramic map**. They were popular in North America during the late nineteenth and early twentieth centuries and were drawn from oblique angles.

This bird's-eye view of Kansas City, Missouri, in 1869 (Figure 7.2) shows the river traffic and the streets laid out in a grid. How much of an area is visible in a bird's-eye map? How do features in the distance change in perspective? How is this view different from a flat map of the same region? How is the horizon part of the view?

Students can compare a panoramic map with a flat map of the same region.

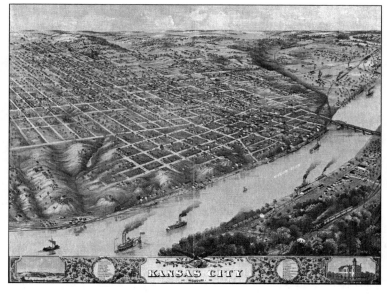

Figure 7.2

Bird's-eye view of Kansas City, Missouri
Source: The Library of Congress

Styles of Maps *(cont.)*

Political maps are human-made drawings of imaginary boundaries between countries, states, counties, and school districts, and they are the most familiar style of maps students study. The lines on political maps are drawn based on legal agreements among nations and regions and can change from time to time. **Topographical maps**, however, show the physical features of an area, region, or the world. Many maps and globes combine physical features and political boundaries.

Some **resource maps** feature pictures or icons pertaining to a particular subject. For example, illustrated maps show locations of all national parks, baseball fields, industries, or oil wells. Other resource maps may label specific sites and then describe those sites in a table on the map. Figure 7.3 is an archaeological map of Iraq designed in 1967. It details all the historical and religious sites where antiquities were located. How were those sites changed during Saddam Hussein's reign? How will an antiquities' map appear after the Iraq War? In what part of Iraq are the most antiquities located?

Some maps can be categorized as **transportation maps** showing railroad lines, city streets, highways stretching across states, or aviation routes. Tourist maps show directions to specific sites and give added details. Figure 7.4 is a railroad map of Iowa. The railroads are colored and labeled. Who would use this map?

Figure 7.3

Archaeological map of Iraq
Source: The Library of Congress

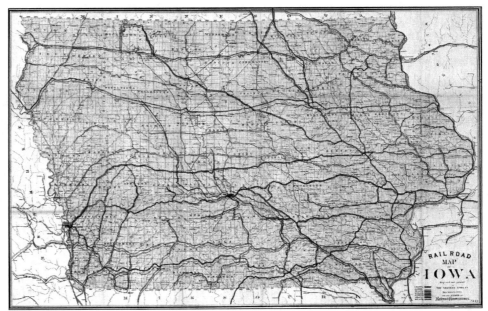

Figure 7.4
Railroad map of Iowa
Source: The Library of Congress

Styles of Maps *(cont.)*

Military maps provide information for a special purpose and may include battle plans drawn in detail. **Weather maps** show past patterns of weather or satellite views of current conditions. **Relief maps** are textural and are usually designed for display purposes. Some relief maps add buildings, bridges, and other human-made structures. **Survey maps** provide valuable information to contractors and developers and are used to establish boundaries for a variety of reasons. **Time zone maps** show human-made lines indicating all the time zones around the world or across a specific area. There are even maps and globes of the ocean's topography and currents.

This CIA-created map (Figure 7.5) focuses on the Indian Ocean. Why would the Central Intelligence Agency be interested in cartography?

Some maps are very narrow in focus. They may depict a neighborhood, a campground, a small tourist area, or a theme park. There are even maps of prisons. This is a map of Dachau Concentration Camp during the Holocaust (Figure 7.6). A United States Army medical officer sketched the map in 1945. Why would the medical officer want to make this map?

Figure 7.5

Map of the Indian Ocean—United States CIA
Source: The Library of Congress

Locating Maps for Classroom Use

There are many modern maps at the CIA World Factbook website (http://www.cia.gov/cia/publications/factbook/). Every country in the world is described in statistical detail and maps are available for countries, continents, regions, oceans, and so on. The Library of Congress has an extensive map collection and the National Archives has maps from all regions and eras in American history. County historical societies contain maps that explain the geographical changes in your city or county. State archives store maps that show changes in state political boundaries. Themed museums have maps that tell about different historical eras. The Internet has vast collections of maps that will suit all areas of your curriculum.

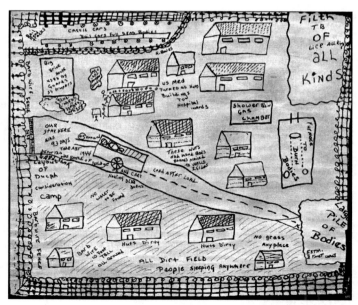

Figure 7.6

Map of Dachau
Source: Unknown medical army officer in 1945

Brief History of Cartography

Since the earliest times, people have constructed maps to explain their environments or to provide a graphic set of directions to get from one place to another. Mapmaking is considered a skilled technology, and today's maps are generated with advanced computer programs. Early man also used the technology he had available by scratching sketches onto leather, wood, parchment, bone, or on the walls of caves.

The first known "map" is a wall painting discovered in Turkey that dates from around 6000 B.C. Another ancient map is a clay tablet found in Iraq and dated around 2300 B.C. The map depicts a man's estate nestled in a valley with mountains on each side. Figure 7.7 shows this ancient map as well as a modern drawing that indicates what is on the clay tablet.

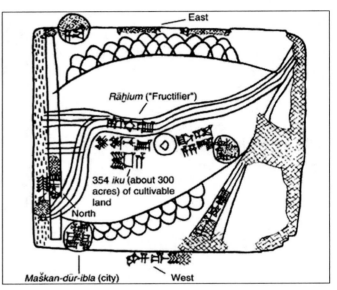

Figure 7.7
Ancient clay tablet
Source: Semitic Museum, Harvard University

The Egyptians made maps as early as 1300 B.C. The Greeks designed maps that showed projection and a type of longitude and latitude as early as 300 B.C. The Greek philosopher and scientist, Aristotle, developed the theory that the earth was round and years later, Ptolemy drew the first world map. Romans used maps to keep track of their vast holdings, to collect taxes in a systematic manner, and to provide strategy for military campaigns. The Romans developed a far-reaching road system and they created maps that detailed those roads as well.

The leaders of the Christian church during the Middle Ages also designed maps, but their purpose was religious rather than scientific. They drew Jerusalem in the center, added the Garden of Eden, and placed east at the top of the map. One such map, created in about 1300, was titled "Hereford Mappa Mundi," since it was produced for the Hereford Cathedral in England. Muslim geographers also produced maps. Al-Idrisi was a Muslim scholar in the court of King Roger II of Sicily, who was a Christian. The unique friendship between these men during the time of the Crusades enabled them to analyze extensive geographical theories and exploration notes. They compiled a book on geography and cartography. Al-Idrisi designed a map of the known world in the twelfth century, drawing south at the top.

Brief History of Cartography *(cont.)*

The first mapmaker to depict the world as a spherical shape was the Greek mathematician Claudius Ptolemy, who wrote an eight-volume geographical encyclopedia in the second century. He drew a map of Earth on a flat surface showing the earth's curve—placing north at the top of the map, east at the right side, and west at the left side. He divided the world map into lines of latitude and longitude. He labeled about 8,000 places on his map.

For over a thousand years, Ptolemy's maps were forgotten until the early fifteenth century when the first copies of his newly discovered maps appeared. His maps were then printed in Bologna, Italy, in 1477. He brought mapmaking to the age of the Renaissance, inspiring Christopher Columbus and other explorers to seek western routes to the East. The map below (Figure 7.8) is one of the early versions of a world map based on the observations of Ptolemy. The map stretches from Britain in the west to Asia in the east, omitting the Americas altogether and only showing about one-third of Africa. This version was made before the information gathered from the voyages of Columbus was officially reported.

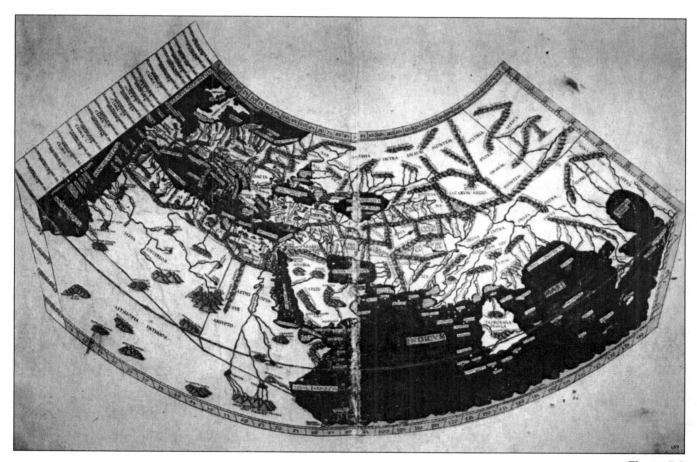

Figure 7.8
Map by Claudius Ptolemy
Source: The Library of Congress

Assignment: Design a class discussion covering questions like the following: Why would mapmakers in the fifteenth century and early sixteenth century want to copy Ptolemy's map? Why hadn't map making improved in over a 1,000 years since his first map was made?

Map Projections

When we study a flat world map in a classroom in the United States, we find North and South America in the center. Students in Europe study world maps that have Europe in the center, while students in Australia study maps with Australia in the center. It is typical for people to place their own countries or environments at the center of their maps as the point of reference. Because Earth is a sphere, it is easy to change perspectives and still be accurate.

Perspective and projections are not the same. The word *projection* comes from the idea of using a transparent globe with a shining light inside which then projects the image of the globe onto a flat surface. Actually, a cartographer mathematically works out the map projections on a flat pattern of meridians and parallels. In reality, it is impossible to make a flat map of a round world that shows all distances, continents, areas, and directions as accurately as a globe does. Any flat map has a certain level of distortion. There are several types of projections within these three categories: azimuthal, cylindrical, and conic. However, the most popular has been a cylindrical projection known as the Mercator projection.

In 1554, Gerardius Mercator produced a six-panel map of Europe. Fourteen years later, he designed a new way of displaying a map with 90-degree parallel lines for the latitudes and meridians. Although he was not the first to try this type of map projection, Mercator was the first cartographer to construct a map using the concept. The Mercator projection (Figure 7.9) was a more accurate guide for navigators to use on sea voyages and gave educated citizens a new concept of the world. However, the Mercator maps showed distortions of areas near the poles in order to get the curvature that was needed. Greenland, for instance, appears 16 times larger than it really is. Mercator produced a three-volume world atlas, which was published in several editions from 1585 to 1594 and added the word *atlas* to the English vocabulary. Future generations of mapmakers, for the most part, took their ideas of mapmaking from Mercator's world atlas.

About 20 years ago, the National Geographic Society and many other mapmakers began using a different projection called the Robinson projection, which slightly distorts various geographical areas to produce a more pleasing world map. The new version does not show Greenland being so dramatically out of proportion. Within the last few years, another similar projection called Winkel Tripel has been the preferred version. It, too, uses subtle distortions throughout the world map, rather than the huge exaggeration of one or two continents.

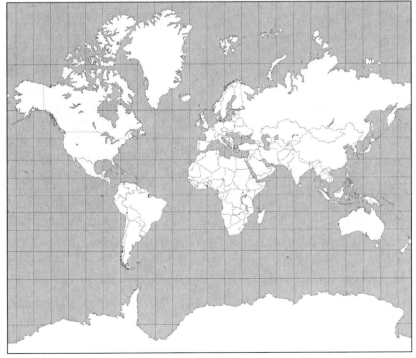

Figure 7.9

Mercator projection map

World Maps

In 1507, a group of European scholars designed an extraordinary world map that included the new discoveries of Columbus and other explorers as a new continent separate from Asia. The cartographer was Martin Waldseemüller. His map (Figure 7.10) was the first to record the New World and to name America in honor of Amerigo Vespucci. The map had been hidden in a German monastery for nearly 80 years until the Library of Congress bought it for over $12,000,000. Waldseemüller's map is now available at the Library of Congress. Their resolution system allows viewers to scan the map and zoom in on parts they want to see in more detail.

Assignment: Using the questions on page 118, decide which ones would be appropriate for Waldseemüller's map.

As explorers gained and shared knowledge about our world, cartographers redrew maps to keep up with the new information. Throughout Europe, maps became "hot-ticket" items for sale, and wealthy men could not wait for the latest world map edition to be published so that they could purchase the ornate copies for their libraries.

Figure 7.10
1507 map by Martin Waldseemüller
Source: The Library of Congress

Mapmakers of the era were not only mathematicians and cartographers, but they were also professional artists. In John Speed's map (Figure 7.11), he shows a double hemisphere perspective and adds astronomical images and mythological figures. It is the first world map in the first English world atlas, which was published in 1676, after Speed's death. It details all the information gathered by Spanish, Portuguese, and English explorers. A group of students could spend a long time analyzing this elaborate map.

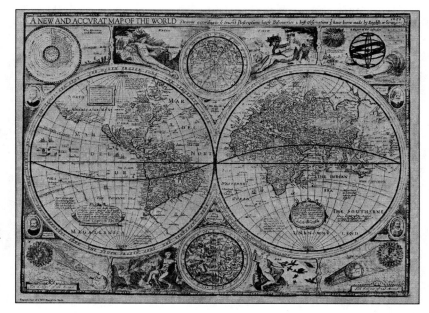

Figure 7.11
1651 Map by John Speed
Source: Historical Documents, Co.

World Maps *(cont.)*

In 1719, Hermon Moll, a Dutch cartographer who lived in London, designed a new world map based on the latest data received from explorers and settlers (Figure 7.12). This elaborate map is very accurate in some regions and very inaccurate in others. What areas are correct and what are incorrect? Most explorations were focused on coastal regions. Since few people had entered the interior of Africa or North and South America, Moll had to make reasonable guesses about these areas.

Assignment: Compare and contrast the Speed map (Figure 7.11) with the Moll map (Figure 7.12). What changes do you notice from 1676 to 1719? Why were the changes needed? Are the two maps different in style? Explain. Both maps are embellished and have added small inserts with extra information. What is the difference in the kinds of information provided?

Mathew Carey's world map (Figure 7.13) includes North and South America and Australia in 1795. The map has two global views, like the John Speed map (Figure 7.11)

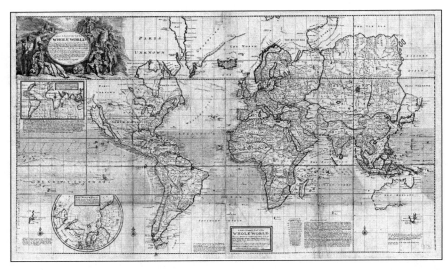

Figure 7.12
A map of the world in 1719 by Hermon Moll
Source: The Library of Congress

Assignment: Compare the two maps on this page. What discoveries had been made and what political events had occurred between the dates of these maps? Write six questions for these maps.

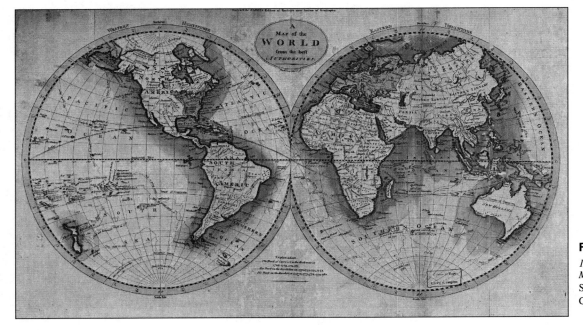

Figure 7.13
1795 map of world by Mathew Carey
Source: The Library of Congress

Early American Maps

In 1585, John White, a British explorer and artist, joined an expedition to America and explored what is now the Carolina coast that Walter Raleigh had named Virginia (including modern-day Virginia, North Carolina, Maryland, Delaware, and Washington, D.C.). White constructed this map (Figure 7.14) detailing the area they were exploring and published his maps when he returned to Great Britain.

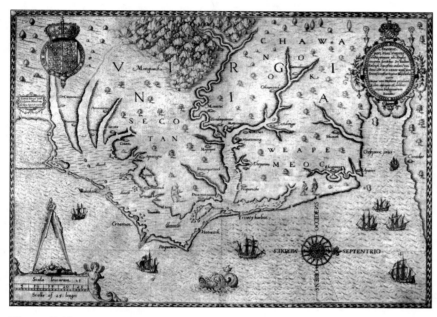

Figure 7.14

John White's map of Virginia
Source: The Library of Congress

Assignment: Students will find it interesting to study the varied symbols on the map and the way White showed topographical features. Maps of this era have embellishments that added artistic flare so that map collectors would purchase copies for their libraries. Design a set of questions about this map's artistic features.

John Smith, Jamestown's leader, was also a brilliant mapmaker. His map of the coastal area of Chesapeake Bay (Figure 7.15) covers 150 miles (241 km). Students should notice that most of the names are related to American Indian tribes in the area.

Assignment: Develop a set of questions for students to answer while using magnifying glasses. Students should analyze the map's geographical areas, notice the names the artist gave each feature, and then discuss the embellishments and their value. Why are the names written in Latin when John Smith was English? Help students to understand and appreciate the talents of people years ago who constructed maps as they explored new regions. What skills would have been needed and what tools would have been used?

Figure 7.15

John Smith's map of colonial America
Source: Historical Documents, Co.

Early American Maps *(cont.)*

George Washington spent his early years surveying and mapping regions around Virginia. This map (Figure 7.16) accompanied his 1754 journal. It includes a graph in the upper left-hand corner and a handwritten description. What other features does he include?

During the two-year interim between the official end of the Revolutionary War and the Treaty of Paris, General Washington requested surveys to provide accurate information for the new government. This map of York and Gloucester (Figure 7.17) was prepared by Sebastian Bauman, a major in the New York or 2nd Regiment of Artillery, who surveyed the region October 22–28, 1781. The survey describes the York River watershed. What are the notes on the left and right of this map? What is the purpose of the large written area at the bottom of the page? What artistic elements were added to this survey? What events were happening 1782?

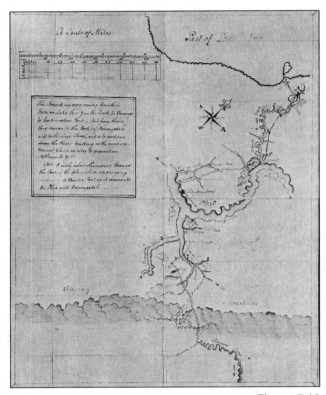

Figure 7.16

Washington's survey map
Source: The Library of Congress

These two maps are available in the American Memory collection of the Library of Congress (http://memory.loc.gov/ammem/). Using their system to view these maps allows viewers to zoom in on specific sections and magnify the map features and writing. Some sections of these maps are best viewed this way. Take time to show students how to search the Library of Congress American Memory collection and how to use the zooming tools.

Figure 7.17

Sebastian Bauman's map for General Washington
Source: The Library of Congress

Early American Maps *(cont.)*

In order to create a new country, boundaries must be established. A legal agreement involves surveys from authorities that all parties agree are acceptable. This map published in London in 1783 (Figure 7.18) depicts the new United States of America determined by the best authorities and agreeable to the peace of 1783, making it one of the first official maps of the new United States.

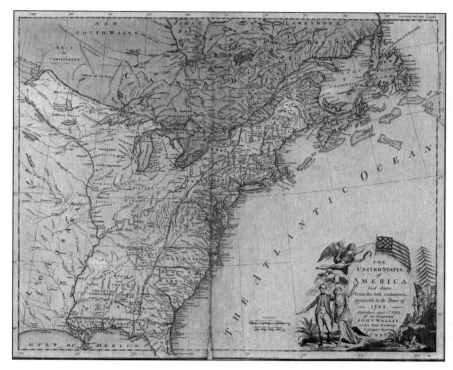

Lewis and Clark's exploration twenty years later would add new information to expand mapmaking across the continent. Numerous maps and sketches from this epic journey are available in the materials prepared for the bicentennial of their expedition.

Figure 7.18

1783 map of the United States of America
Source: The Library of Congress

Territorial maps are also interesting map studies. The map of the Oklahoma Indian Territory (Figure 7.19) could be used in the study of American Indians, the history of the Oklahoma Run, or an exploration of westward expansion. Students can compare this map to a modern map of the same region.

Assignment: Examine both maps using the steps listed in the overview of this chapter.

Figure 7.19

Oklahoma Territory map
Source: The Library of Congress

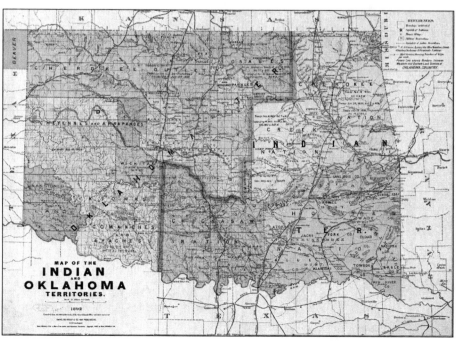

Model Lessons and Activities

On the next few pages, you will find two model lessons using maps. Each lesson provides objectives, activities, and creative ideas.

Maps Model Lesson for Grades 4–8

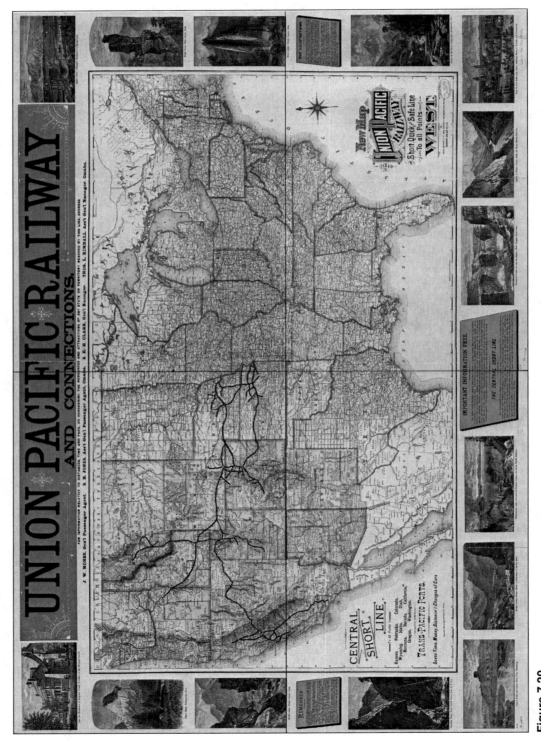

Figure 7.20
The Union Pacific Railway map
Source: The Library of Congress

Model Lessons and Activities *(cont.)*

Maps Model Lesson for Grades 4–8 *(cont.)*

Objectives

- Students will study the different regions shown on this map to determine what areas the railroad passed through on its route west. They will also find out what the scenic points of interest along that route were.

- Students will analyze the various features of a railway, advertising poster.

Background Information

On May 10, 1869, at Promontory Summit, Utah, the Central Pacific Railroad joined the Union Pacific Railroad to form the first Transcontinental Railroad. Soon building supplies, merchandise for sale, livestock, and passengers were traveling the rails. It was finally possible to travel from New York to California in 10 days rather than in many months. People began to think of traveling for pleasure not just for migration. The Union Pacific Railway began promoting vacation trips by train through scenic sections of the country that had once been difficult to cross.

Teaching Strategies

1. Distribute copies of the Union Pacific Railway (Figure 7.20) map. This map is also provided on the CD for your use (filename: railway.jpg).

2. Be a map detective. Using a magnifying glass or hand lens, answer the following questions:

   - What types of scenic places are shown around the outside of this map? Do you recognize any of these?

   - Look over the map to see if any states were different in 1883 than they are today. Write the names of the ones you find.

   - What does the logo on the right say about the Union Pacific Railway? What kind of advertising technique is this logo? What does the logo on the left say about the Central Short Line?

   - What type of information is given under the title? Why is that important?

Extension Activity

Using the format of this map, that features a border of tourist sites, design a map for your state. Draw a map of your state in the middle and then either draw or cut and paste pictures of special tourist sites around the perimeter of your state. Write a few catchy statements (or slogans) to use on the map that will make prospective tourists want to come to your state.

Model Lessons and Activities *(cont.)*

Maps Model Lesson for Grades 9–12

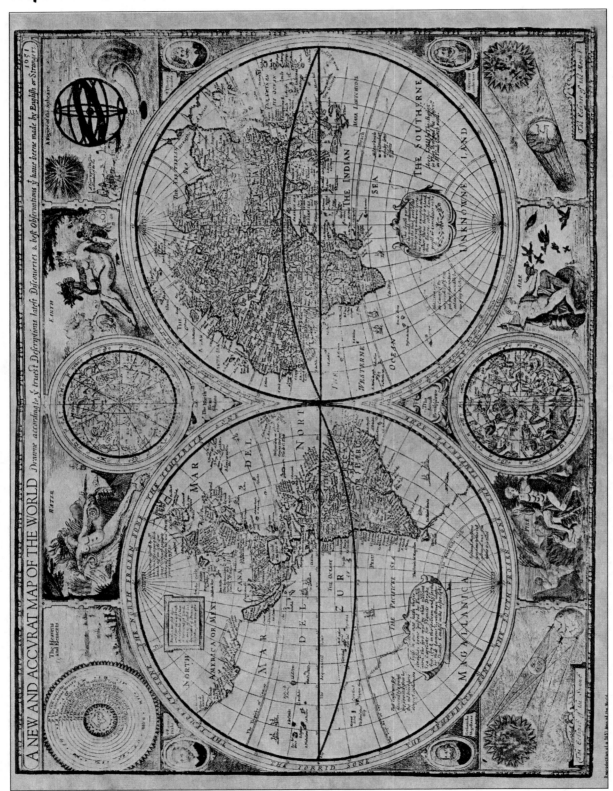

Figure 7.21
John Speed's New and Accurate Map of the World
Source: Historical Documents, Co.

Model Lessons and Activities *(cont.)*

Maps Model Lesson for Grades 9–12 *(cont.)*

Objectives

- Students will analyze the viewpoints of mapmakers and will note the exploration discoveries that mapmakers might include in their seventeenth-century maps.

- Students will analyze the various features on an ancient world map and compare its features to a modern-day world map.

Teaching Strategies

1. Distribute copies of Speed's World Map (Figure 7.21). This map is also provided on the CD for your use (filename: speed.jpg).

2. Lead the students in a class discussion using these questions:

   - Why is this map much more elaborate than a modern-day world map?

   - Why would the four elements (fire, water, air, and earth) be significant on a seventeenth century map?

   - Just glancing at the two hemispheres, what do you notice is different in each hemisphere from today's maps?

3. Have students examine the map using magnifying glasses or hand lenses and answer these questions:

   - Make a list of the seas and oceans in both hemispheres as shown on this map. Which names have changed since this map was created?

   - Name the continents on this map. Which continent is missing? Why? Which continents are the least accurate by today's standards?

   - What do the three other circular maps depict? Why would the artist add these?

   - What men are featured in the four cameos? What moon/sun projections did the artist include? What does the geometric sphere in the right corner represent?

   - Write four more questions about this map that you would like to have answered.

4. Using the *Comparing Views of the World Chart* (page 134), compare and contrast this map with a modern one.

Model Lessons and Activities *(cont.)*

Maps Model Lesson for Grades 9–12 *(cont.)*

- -

Name_____

Comparing Views of the World Chart

Directions: Write your observations for each map and compare and contrast the parts of both maps listed below.

	John Speed Map	Modern Map
Number of continents		
Lines of latitude and longitude		
North America		
Names of oceans		
Tropic of Cancer and Tropic of Capricorn		
West Indies		
Embellishments		

General Analysis Strategies

These strategies can be used with any maps. Students can:

- Compare an antique map with a modern map of the same area.

- Take modern-day maps, cut them out, paste them on poster paper, and then add artistic details to their maps in a similar style to the antique maps.

- Find three or four different styles of maps for the same region. For example, students can use a bird's-eye view of Kansas City, an aerial map of Kansas City, a road map of Kansas City, and a political map of Kansas City. Ask students to compare what kinds of information they can get from each style. Which style do they prefer?

- Research the biographies of different cartographers and give presentations about the cartographers of their choice.

- Find four panoramic maps and compare how the artists interpreted the area in each map. What seems to be the focal point in each map? Why was that focal point chosen?

- Work in groups of four to divide maps into four segments and write analyses of the segments. Some groups may decide to divide their maps into four parallel segments and others may divide their maps into four rectangles formed by folding the paper in the middle both ways.

- Ask a member of your local historical society or archives to bring an old map of the area where your school is now located. The map should have been made before the school was built. Have students study what that area looked like 50 or more years ago and have students make lists of their observations.

- Invite a cartographer to your classroom to explain how maps are made in today's economy.

- Find four different maps of your state or city to cover time periods that are each at least 30 years apart. Then, they can compare and contrast the areas of all four maps and write their observations. Finally, they can make posters showcasing the four maps and write descriptions of their observations.

- Choose continents to research online. They can find maps from the fifteenth century through the twenty-first century and then make illustrated and captioned poster displays about how the continents have been interpreted in map form over time.

Notes

Artifacts

Overview

In addition to documents, photographs, prints, and maps, historians also use artifacts to interpret history. Artifacts are formally defined as "objects of material cultural." Holding or viewing an artifact puts us in a more intimate relationship with those that used or owned the object in the past. This physical relationship spurs an interest in how and when the object was used. Obviously, most artifacts associated with famous people or famous events are found in museums or owned by specialized collectors. The artifacts pictured in Figure 8.1 were those items found in Lincoln's pockets upon his assassination. Seeing these objects in a museum display brings students back to that fateful night.

Figure 8.1

The contents of Abraham Lincoln's pockets on the night of his assassination, April 14, 1865
Source: The Library of Congress

In some cases, museums make replicas of these objects for students to hold, manipulate, and study. For the most part, genuine artifacts that belonged to everyday people will be the objects that students get to hold and examine. Kitchen utensils from the turn of the century, serving pieces from the Victorian era, a stereoscope and slides used in parlors of the past, old hat boxes, and vintage clothing will be available from friends, relatives, or from the family members of your students.

Artifacts can also become part of your classroom experience by inviting an antique dealer to visit your class and bring objects that match the era you are studying. Some dealers would welcome the opportunity to introduce the younger generation to the pleasures of antiquing. Some students may already be quite articulate about the value of certain collectible items. One enjoyable activity is to bring in artifacts that require students to guess their purposes. For example, you could bring in the removable 45-spindle insert on a record player. That will stump most students who cannot imagine what the item might be. Tools from the 1800s, such as the gauge in Figure 8.2, can also keep students guessing.

Figure 8.2
Gauge
Source: The National Frontier Trails Museum

Overview *(cont.)*

Artifacts may be classified by usage rather than by types of materials. Clothing; tools; furnishings; storage containers; cooking and eating utensils; communication devices; transportation devices; clocks and watches; money; nautical, astronomical, and mathematical instruments; weapons; and ornamental objects are some of the classifications. In what category would you classify each of these items?

Figure 8.3a
Bonnet
Source: The National Frontier Trails Museum

Figure 8.3b
Powder horn
Source: The National Frontier Trails Museum

Figure 8.3c
Coffee mill
Source: The National Frontier Trails Museum

Figure 8.3d
Packsaddle
Source: The National Frontier Trails Museum

General Questions and Activities

In order to understand or appreciate many artifacts, students need background information about the object's history or purpose. When students first look at the iron circle with a brand-name cut out (Figure 8.4), they might think it is a company plaque to hang on the wall or door. However, with background information, students will know it is a stencil that fits over the top of a flour barrel. A company painter could quickly stencil the company's name on the barrel's top, keeping him from having to handwrite the name on each lid.

The marking gauge shown in Figure 8.5 measures the circumference of an object such as a barrel. So, both of these artifacts would have been used by settlers in the West.

Figure 8.4

Waggoner Gates Milling Co. iron stencil
Source: The National Frontier Trails Museum

Figure 8.5

Marking gauge
Source: The National Frontier Trails Museum

Here are some questions you could ask students about historical artifacts.

- In which general category does this object belong—clothing; tools; furnishings; storage containers; cooking and eating utensils; communication devices; transportation devices; time pieces; money; nautical, astronomical, and mathematical instruments; weapons; or ornamental objects?

- How was the item constructed? What materials were used?

- What is the shape, texture, color, size, weight, dimensions, movable parts, and odor of this object?

- Does the item have any writing? What does the writing mean?

- Was the item handmade or manufactured? What is the quality of the construction of the item?

- Who would have used the item?

- What was the item's purpose?

- Could this item still be useful today? Why or why not?

- What does this item reveal about the technology of the era in which it was made?

- What modern object has a similar function to this object?

- Do you think this item had a patent? Why or why not?

General Questions and Activities *(cont.)*

Assign one of the following for your students to complete:

- Write a character sketch of a person who might have used this item.

- Write a character sketch of a person who might have made this item.

- Pretend you are a museum curator. Write a description of the item for a display case.

- Write a story about the item using personification by pretending that you are the item and telling your story from a first-person point of view. For example: You are a spinning wheel from the 1820s. Who made you? How were you used? Where have you been since then? Be creative but accurate in your details.

- Explain how this item fits into our current study in social studies? What does it reveal about the people of that era?

- Check an antique catalog to see if this item is listed. What did you find out?

Ideas for Classroom Projects and Displays

Making a Classroom Museum

Students can prepare different museums to show their understanding of special areas of study. They can create museums with teams of students responsible for designing the displays, constructing the replica artifacts, preparing the multimedia shows, and conducting tours. Students are responsible for the labeling of displays and for developing tour information. Students become tour guides for the displays if you invite other classes to your museum. Or, your students can proudly tour their families through their museum. When your class visits a museum, they will be much more attentive because they understand both the work that goes into making displays and the responsibilities of being a tour guide.

Communication Artifacts Display Table

Students will love creating a communication artifacts display table. First, you have to collect the artifacts. Beg, borrow, or buy at garage sales the following items: rotary dial telephone, old wooden wall telephone, small 45-RPM record player, super-eight movie camera, old box camera, 45-RPM record player spindle that was inserted over a 78-RMP spindle, IBM punch cards, reel-to-reel movie projector, old manual typewriter, reel-to-reel tape player, pictures of telephone operators on the job, picture of an old Victrola and the records that were used with it, pictures of early computers that were the size of refrigerators, and any other items that are considered artifacts.

Students should gather around the table in groups. They can handle and discuss the objects and pictures to gather the information they think they know about each one. Students then move the objects into categories. They can organize the items by the correct era. They can order the items from oldest to newest. They can select all items from one communication category and put them in order of age. They can select two items and research the history of each item as if they were cataloging the item for a museum.

Discuss with students that some of these items were used for many years, without any changes made to the product. Have the students compare the changes in communication in their lifetimes with the communication changes during previous decades. What have been the key factors in the communication revolution in the last 10 years? What is the most modern item on the table? What is the most basic item on the table? Why? How did the microchip change communication devices? What is the modern counterpart to each item on this table?

Ideas for Classroom Projects and Displays *(cont.)*

One Teacher's Story

Keil Hileman, a social studies teacher from Monticello Trails Middle School in Shawnee Mission, Kansas, has developed the idea of using artifacts to turn his classroom into an amazing "classroom museum." He was selected the 2004 Kansas Teacher of the Year and was one of four finalists for National Teacher of the Year. Hileman uses primary sources and artifacts as the basis for teaching social studies. His room is full of 20,000 authentic and replica artifacts, arranged by categories in artful vignettes (Figures 8.6 and 8.7). He makes these comments about his experiences using artifacts:

> I have found that the best approach to teaching the social sciences is a visual and hands-on methodology. Once you have started a collection of teaching artifacts in your room, the collection will grow through student-created projects and donations from outside sources (i.e., parents, grandparents, or church groups). Your students will learn and enjoy your lessons more than before. Quite frankly, we live in an age of spectacular visual and physical experiences. Having students surrounded by artifacts that teach is the best way I have found to motivate and educate students.

> My students look forward to being in my class. They never know what new items they will see and learn about each day. This anticipation is invaluable as an instructional tool. Students will work harder to get to your room on time. Students will be more motivated to get through with homework, quizzes, and exams in order to reach project times, "show and tell," or "pass-around" days. The museum artifacts can be used to motivate students to finish their work early. You can even use the artifacts as rewards for good behavior. All you have to do is have things they want to touch, explore, and examine in your room.

Hileman includes both authentic artifacts and replicas of artifacts in his classroom museum. Students know the difference, but it is still fun to handle a reproduction of a knight's helmet even if it is not the real thing! Students also make replicas of artifacts; build models of buildings; design dioramas of historic events and scenes; and help set up museum-style displays in his classroom. The classroom is therefore a living museum with real artifacts, models, displays, and stored objects. Students feel ownership of the classroom and cherish the items since they must keep them safe and tidy.

Figure 8.6

Keil Hileman's classroom

Figure 8.7

Keil Hileman's classroom

Getting Artifacts for Your Classroom

Collecting items from different cultures can also give students a greater understanding of how others live, act, celebrate, and raise their families. Keil Hileman suggests the following:

There are three main ways to gather artifacts. You can always buy artifacts from antique stores, garage sales, friends, catalogs, on the Internet, and anywhere else you see something that would support your curriculum. You may want to seek financial support from local businesses, the PTO/PTA, or organizations that focus on history. Once your reputation has spread throughout the community, people may also seek your classroom museum as a resting place for artifacts their families no longer value. Many families will sell or donate items when relatives pass away. Military veterans often say that donating items to our classroom museum is a way to connect younger generations to the past. I have many World War II veterans who have donated amazing things to remind my students about that war. One amazing item was a Nazi banner including a swastika.

Figure 8.8

Keil Hileman's classroom

Classroom Activities Using Artifacts by Keil Hileman

- **Touch Tables**—Take all of the artifacts that are connected to the current area of study and keep them out on a table while the unit is being taught. Students are free to read about them, touch them, and study them.

- **Open Discussion and Analysis**—Present an item that the students have not seen before and have them guess what it might be, how it was used, and why it is significant to the topic of discussion. It is a great way to start a unit.

- **Topics for Research**—Present a carefully chosen item, give students a few clues about the item, and send them on a research-gathering adventure.

- **Cleaning and Restoration**—Through the process of cleaning new and old acquisitions, students learn about the construction and purpose of different items.

- **Identification and Explanation Assessments**—Take all of the artifacts that have been used during the teaching of a unit and use them in the exam. This can be done orally or in a myriad of written methods. List the items and have the students define them from memory and in their own words. They will need to explain how the items were used, who used them, and identify to which period in history the artifacts belong.

- **Drama Props**—Any play or drama skit can be a great opportunity to utilize your artifacts and get them in the students' and parents' view.

- **Cultural Examples**—If you collect the right type of artifacts, they can be the best source of information about cultures and their defining values. The most common question students seem to have about another cultures is, "Why do they do that?" Analyzing and studying a good artifact or two from that culture often helps answer that kind of question.

- **Memory Triggers**—By simply being surrounded by all of these visual artifacts, students are continually exposed to the history they are studying. Students will often look around the room during tests and see an artifact that will "trigger" a memory and help them with the test. You can answer questions during exams by reminding students to go look at a key artifact. You will enjoy seeing the "light bulb" come on when they smile and say, "Now I remember!"

- **Museum Night**—Plan a Museum Night and have student volunteers dress up in historical costumes and become museum ambassadors. In my class, each volunteer was responsible for a small section of the room and came to a few practice sessions to review the information about the artifacts in their areas. During the evening, I had the parent group provide coffee, punch, and cookies. All 180 guests signed the guest book and recorded their comments after seeing the museum. Many of these guests had donated or purchased items for the museum. This night did more to get the word out about the museum than I could have ever imagined.

These ideas were used with permission from Keil Hileman.

Model Lesson and Activity

On the next few pages, you will find a model lesson using artifacts. The lesson provides objectives, activities, and creative ideas.

Artifacts Model Lesson for Grades 3–4 or 5–8

This lesson can be adapted for any grade level simply by altering the levels of questions and kinds of activities.

Objectives

- Students will understand that all countries have monetary systems and that their coins reflect their system and have inscriptions that indicate special symbols in their country's heritage.

- **Grades 3–4:** Students will sort coins according to their sizes and shapes. They will observe their coins and answer questions about how they look. They will make generalizations about their coins.

- **Grades 5–8:** Students will sort coins according to their countries of origin. They will observe their coins and answer questions about how they look. They will make generalizations about their coins and do follow-up research about one set of coins to determine the names and values in U.S. dollars.

Teaching Strategies

1. You will need a variety of foreign coins; metric rulers; and small gram scales. Now that many European countries are using the Euro, you may need to find older coins for this lesson. Because so many people travel to distant countries, you will want to ask family members, friends, families of students, and so on to save coins from their trips and to donate them to your coin artifact collection. Be on the lookout for older United States coins and commemorative state coins to add to your collection.

1. Divide students into groups. Pass out a random collection of foreign coins to each group. According to the age group, have students sort coins by one of the objectives above.

2. This is an exploration of common artifacts that we all encounter. Let the students explore the collections without giving added information at this time. There should be lots of group discussion. Students may realize that country names are on the coins or they may notice that some coins have similar symbols.

3. When they have finished sorting, pass out the appropriate activity sheet (page 147 or 148) for each grade level. Each activity sheet has tasks for examining the coins.

4. When the groups have finished the activity sheets, spend time describing the different countries represented.

Model Lesson and Activity *(cont.)*

Artifacts Model Lesson for Grades 3–4 or 5–8 *(cont.)*

Name: _____

We're in the Money! Grades 3–4

Directions: Each group member gets a task sheet. Each group should get metric rulers and a gram scale. Look at your coins.

1. How many sets of coins did you make?

   _____

2. How did you group your coins: by size; by size and shape; by color, etc.

   _____

3. Each group member will choose one coin. Describe the images on each side of your coin.

   _____

4. What numbers are on your coin?

   _____

5. Measure your coin across the middle (diameter). How many centimeters is your coin?

   _____

6. How much does it weigh in grams?

   _____

7. What is the color of your coin (silver, copper, gold, other)?

   _____

8. Write down the words on your coin. Can you understand those words? Do you think the words are in another language? Which one?

   _____

   _____

   _____

9. What country do you think your coin is from?

   _____

10. What did all the coins have in common?

    _____

    _____

Model Lesson and Activity *(cont.)*

Artifacts Model Lesson for Grades 3–4 or 5–8 *(cont.)*

- -

Name_____

We're in the Money! Grades 5–8

Directions: Each group member gets a task sheet. Each group needs metric rulers and a gram scale.

1. How many sets of coins did your group have?

   _____

2. What countries do you think were represented?

   _____

3. How did you decide the country origin of each coin?

   _____

4. What did you notice about the shapes and sizes of these coins in comparison to U.S. coins?

   _____

   _____

   _____

5. Choose one country and identify what symbols were on the coins of that country. Why were those symbols used?

   _____

   _____

   _____

6. Select one coin and respond to the following prompts on another sheet of paper.

   - What is the size (cm)? Shape? Color? Weight?
   - What words are on the coin?
   - What do you think the words mean?
   - What is the value?

   - What is the country of origin?
   - What generalization can you make about all the coins you sorted?

Research Challenge: Find the country your coin represents on the Internet or in other sources. What is their monetary system called? What is the value of their money in U.S. dollars? How much money would this coin be worth in U.S. dollars? Share your findings with the class.

Films and Sound Recordings

Films Overview

Films can be silent or sound movies, animated cartoons, newsreels like those shown at the "picture show" years ago, documentaries, training films, action films, films of famous events or speeches, clips from vintage television shows, commercials, or home movies. Each type of film tells a story of the time in which it was made and the people who are featured in it. Students are drawn to films, since visual images are a major part of their lives. Therefore, it is a natural fit to use films in the classroom to enhance student learning of different historic eras.

The choices you have as a classroom teacher are numerous. Using films, however, can be time consuming in a classroom situation that is already crowded with so many requirements to cover. It is probably more beneficial to get into the "clips" habit. Showing a three- to ten-minute clip of a film that matches your objectives will get your point across and keep the time factor under control. Showing two short clips of an event and comparing and contrasting the different interpretations can be a valuable and eye-opening experience. Strategies for analyzing films can vary based on the type of film your students are viewing and your purposes for having them watch the film.

Here are a few generic questions to consider when teaching with different styles of films.

- What are the film's statistics: name, date, source, type of film?

- If it is a speech, who is the speaker, where was the speech given, and why was the speech given? Is the speech famous as a turning point in history? An example is Dr. Martin Luther King Jr.'s "I Have a Dream" speech. How eloquent is the speaker?

- Who is the intended audience for the film?

- What is the theme of the film?

- Summarize the meaning of the film in three sentences.

- How does this film enhance your understanding of the subject we are studying?

- How are people dressed in the film? What does their clothing tell you about the era in which this film was made?

- How does the film use music to enhance the mood?

- If this is live action, who might be the person filming the event? How does viewing this live action make you feel?

- What is the purpose of the film: to entertain, inform, persuade, or record a memory?

- What types of situations or language in this film would be "politically incorrect" today? Why and how?

- What actions in this film are mild in comparison to how they would be portrayed today? For example, a murder that took place in a 1940s film would not have involved viewing a mangled body; intimacy is suggested not demonstrated; profanity is not spoken—not even by the "bad guys."

Sound Recordings Overview

When Thomas Edison first invented the phonograph, he dreamed of it becoming a popular and necessary piece of equipment in every business and home. It took years before that happened, but American lives were changed when it did happen!

Edison stated the following possible future uses for the phonograph in *North American Review*, June 1878: (Source: The Library of Congress)

Figure 9.1

Phonograph advertisement
Source: The Library of Congress

- Letter writing and all kinds of dictation without the aid of a stenographer

- Phonographic books, which will speak to blind people without effort on their part

- The teaching of elocution

- Reproduction of music

- The "Family Record"— a registry of sayings, reminiscences, the last words of dying persons, etc., by members of a family

- Music boxes and toys

- Clocks that should announce in articulate speech the time for going home, going to meals, etc.

- The preservation of languages by exact reproduction of the manner of pronouncing

- Educational purposes; such as preserving the explanations made by a teacher so that the pupil can refer to them at any moment, and spelling or other lessons placed upon the phonograph for convenience in committing to memory

- Connection with the telephone, so as to make that instrument an auxiliary in the transmission of permanent and invaluable records, instead of being the recipient of momentary and fleeting communication

Sound Recordings Overview *(cont.)*

Sound recordings can include popular music from different eras, radio programs, radio commercials, famous speeches, state of the union addresses, press conferences, family events, interviews, congressional testimonies, or news reports. Figure 9.2 is a poster from 1899 that advertises Edison's phonograph.

Some points to consider when listening to sound recordings are:

- What are the recording's statistics: name, date, type of recording, producer?

- Where was this recorded: studio, at a meeting, in a home?

- Who is the intended audience for the recording?

- What is the theme of the recording?

- Summarize the meaning of the recording in two sentences.

- How does this recording enhance your understanding of the subject we are studying?

- What sound effects, narration, music, or background sounds do you notice?

- What is the purpose of the recording: to entertain, inform, persuade, or record a memory?

- Why was the recording made? Cite evidence from what you hear and perceive.

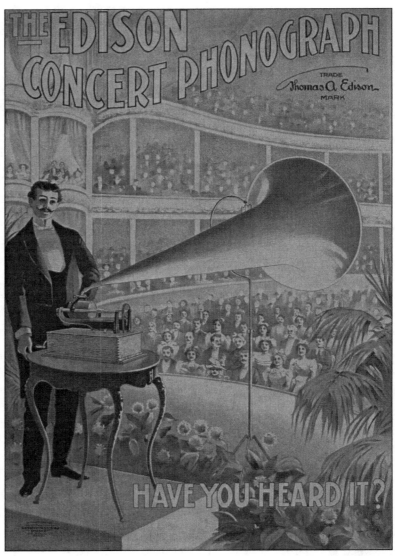

Figure 9.2
The Edison concert phonograph
Source: The Library of Congress

Music

Students eagerly listen to the music of other eras, quickly form their own judgments, and analyze words, melody, and beat. Students enjoy songs from long ago, such as "The Star Spangled Banner" (Figure 9.3), or songs from now. Music from all eras can be used to teach students about daily life throughout history.

Here are some teaching strategies for using historic music in your classroom:

- Students listen to songs from a certain era, the Roaring Twenties, for example. What themes seem to be prevalent in those songs? Are the words easy to understand?

- Students listen to war theme songs from several eras—World War I, World War II, Korea, Vietnam—and discuss whether the lyrics were supportive of the war effort or opposed to it. Why? What is a recurring theme in war songs? How are the songs from the 1960s and 1970s different from the songs of the other war eras?

- Play a variety of songs from different eras and play a game called "Name That Era." Students guess whether the song was from the turn of the century, the 1920s, 1930s, 1940s, etc.

- Students identify the types of instruments being used in a music recording.

- Students determine the styles of a series of different songs: jazz, big band, ballad, silly song, be-bop, rock 'n' roll, etc.

- Have students consider this question: After listening to music from your great-grandparents' or grandparents' era, why do you think it is difficult for them to appreciate the music of teens today? Ask your grandparents if their parents and grandparents also had a hard time understanding their taste in music when they were teens.

Figure 9.3

"The Star Spangled Banner"
Source: The Library of Congress

Commercials—Radio and Television

Commercials can interest students and help them understand the types of products and advertising techniques that were popular in other eras. Here are some questions to use when studying commercials.

- What is being sold: a product, a person (political candidate), or an idea?

- Who made this commercial? When? Where?

- Who was the intended audience?

- What ideas were used to persuade the audience? Were those ideas effective?

- If you had lived in that time, would you have supported the product, candidate, or idea? Why or why not?

- What aspects of the commercial were entertaining?

- Did the commercial have a jingle that helped you remember the product, candidate, or idea?

- Compare this commercial to a modern-day radio or television commercial of the same theme. How are they similar and different?

- Many modern commercials barely mention the product. How many times and ways was the product name mentioned in this commercial? Was it effective or annoying?

Radio and Vintage Television Programs

Many old radio and television programs are available on tape and can be purchased or borrowed for classroom use. Students will find old radio shows, such as *The Shadow, Dragnet, War of the Worlds,* and *George Burns and Gracie Allen,* entertaining and possibly fascinating. The way the producer handled sound effects and transitions between scenes will provide topics of interest for class discussion. Listening to a radio broadcast can involve different skills than watching a vintage television program.

Vintage television programs, such as *The Ed Sullivan Show, I Love Lucy, Red Skelton, Howdy Doody,* and *Dragnet,* will be somewhat familiar to students who watch channels that feature the "oldies." Clips from these and other similar television shows can be an opportunity to discuss cultural and social values of different eras.

These questions can be used for analyzing radio and television programs:

- What is the title of the program? Who produced the program? When did it air?

- Who are the actors? Who is the producer?

- What is the plot? Who are the main characters?

- Summarize the story in a few sentences.

- How does this program relate to our current area of study?

- Was this broadcast part of a series?

- What does the script tell us about the era in which it was written?

- Are there any stereotypes in this program?

- Who are the sponsors for the program?

- Write down all the types of sound or special effects you hear or see, including background noises.

- Imagine a family listening to this broadcast or viewing this television program during its time. What would have been their reactions to the broadcast?

- What type of program is this: drama, comedy, mystery, soap opera, etc.?

Documentaries and Movies

You will receive enthusiastic responses from students who get to spend some class time viewing movie or documentary clips. Documentary clips may be used to define the social structure of an era or region; to define how reporters or the government interpreted the war their countries were waging; to examine a national disaster or tragedy; to recapture a famous event; or to reveal the prejudices, virtues, and viewpoints of a different era. These are good questions to ask about documentaries:

- What is the title of the program? Who produced the program? When did it air?

- What is the purpose of the documentary?

- Summarize the event in a few sentences.

- How does this program relate to our current area of study?

- What does the topic tell us about the era in which it was made?

- Are there any stereotypes in this program?

- Who are the sponsors for the program (news channel, the government, an agency)?

- Imagine a citizen viewing this documentary during its own time. What would have been his or her reaction to the broadcast? What is your reaction to this documentary?

- What are the main points covered in this documentary?

Movie clips from the old West may be shown to demonstrate how stereotypes and myths are reinforced. Students can compare what they are seeing with the facts they have researched about real life in the West. Movie clips from the Great Depression era or World War II era will demonstrate how Hollywood portrayed the time period or supported the war effort. These are good questions to ask about movies:

- What is the title of the movie? Who produced the movie? When was it shown?

- Who are the actors?

- What is the plot? Who are the main characters?

- Summarize the story line in a few sentences.

- How does this movie relate to our current area of study?

- What does the script tell us about the era in which it was written?

- Are there any stereotypes or myths in this movie?

- How does the movie use music and background noise?

- Compare this movie with a contemporary movie of the same genre.

Speeches, Press Conferences, News Reports, and Interviews

Generic questions that can be used when studying speeches, press conferences, news reports, and interviews are listed below.

- What is the title of the speech, interview, or press conference?

- What is the main news story in the news report?

- Who are the speakers or reporters? How eloquent are the speakers or reporters?

- When was the speech, interview, or report made? Where?

- Why was the speech or interview made?

- Who was the intended audience?

- What ideas were used to persuade or inform the audience? Were those ideas effective?

- If you had lived in the time of the recording, would you have supported the statements that were made? Why or why not?

- What aspects of the speech were entertaining, emotional, sad, inspirational, upsetting, depressing, or surprising?

- Write questions about the piece using the Five W's and H: Who? What? When? Where? Why? and How?

- Is the speech famous as a turning point in history? For example, a famous turning-point speech is President Franklin D. Roosevelt's December 1941 speech notifying the American public about the bombing of Pearl Harbor.

Audio Recordings of Speeches, Press Conferences, News Reports, and Interviews

While students may gravitate toward music, commercials, and radio programs, they may have a different attitude when given the assignment of listening to speeches. Audio speeches are difficult to understand, and student concentration may wane because students are more accustomed to the current style of speeches and news reports on television. The following are some activities to help students improve their listening skills.

- Stop the speech at intervals and discuss with students what they heard. Ask students to summarize what was said, or ask them to express how the speech made them feel.

- Rewind a portion of the speech, listen to it a second time, and review the confusing parts.

- Ask students to focus their listening by concentrating on key ideas that you have written on the board.

- Give out cards to students with different points from the speech, and then ask students to raise their cards when they hear the sections spoken.

- Provide the background of the speech in a dramatic manner.

- Give students some hints about what they might hear, but do not give away the "good stuff." Make listening to the speech a mystery-listening assignment in which you give the students some clues and they must listen to find the answers.

- Have students judge the speech based on certain criteria that they have decided on in advance.

- Require students to take notes while listening to the speech. Discuss their notes in groups.

- Invite students to write down questions as they listen to a press conference or interview. What would they have asked the speaker, president, or the interviewee of a press conference or interview if they had been a reporter at the time?

Finding Films and Sound Recordings

To find films and sound recordings, start in your local public libraries. These institutes are treasures of sound and film recordings. Local public libraries have old radio broadcasts, vintage television shows, and famous old movies, and their free-rental policy is an added bonus. It is highly recommended that you schedule well in advance of your show date because recordings are very popular for classroom use. *War of the Worlds* and *Atomic Café* may also available from your local library or can be requested from a partner library. *Atomic Café* is a 1950s collection of government propaganda clips regarding safety procedures in case of a nuclear attack. Old radio and television broadcasts can also be purchased through catalogs and the Internet.

One website that has numerous sound clips of important events is *Sounds of History* (http://www.sinberg.com/~history/). This site has over 300 recordings—some are brief sound bytes and others last over an hour. The variety includes Thomas Edison reciting "Mary Had a Little Lamb," news bulletins, Churchill's speeches, the U.S. Supreme Court case of *Roe v. Wade*, and hundreds more.

Old Time Radio—Radio Days: A Soundbite History (http://www.otr.com) is a rich source of nostalgic and old time radio series and news. Mysteries, spy shows, science fiction, comedy, and action series are available. The sound recordings are clear and can be played directly through the computer.

History Place—Sounds of Presidents (http://www.historyplace.com/specials/sounds-prez/) contains mini-sound bytes of presidential speeches and announcements.

Remembering the 1940s (http://www.1940.co.uk) supplies the British perspective of World War II in sound, documents, and articles.

American Rhetoric (http://www.americanrhetoric.com/) has a series of famous speeches both as recordings and as written transcripts.

You can also purchase collections of films, movies, and vintage television shows at your local video stores, large retail chains, or on the Internet.

Model Lesson and Activity

Film and Sound Recordings Model Lesson for Grades 6–12

Objectives

- Students will read, listen to, and discuss Martin Luther King Jr.'s "I Have a Dream" speech. Students will discuss what makes the speech a landmark in American history.

- Students will listen to a speech while reading along with their own transcripts. They will analyze the speech's content through analogies, metaphors, and visual images.

Teaching Strategies

1. Discuss ahead of time the background of the speech, the location, and the event that was taking place. Explain why the speech is a landmark speech in our nation's history. Explain that great speeches inspire by using visual images, metaphors, and analogies.

2. Provide students with written copies of the full speech that Dr. King delivered August 28, 1963, at the Lincoln Memorial in Washington, D.C. Play the entire recording (which can be accessed online or through another source such as your school library) while students follow along with their written copies of the speech.

3. Explain to the students that they will be listening to the speech and following along with written copies. Provide a short list of tasks for students to do as they listen. Review their responses to these tasks at the end of each pause in the speech.
   - Put an X after each sentence that made the audience cheer.
   - Underline any important image, metaphor, or analogy that Dr. King used to make his point.
   - Circle the word *freedom* or *free* each time it is used in the text.
   - Underline the word *dream* twice each time it is used.

4. Students will listen to the speech and follow along with their own copies of the speech. Play the recording, and then stop the recording at intervals, asking students to share what phrases they have underlined, words they have circled or underlined, and where they have placed the Xs. Lead a class discussion of the content and style. On the next page is a list of places to stop the tape and questions to use for class discussion.

Extension Activity

After this analysis, have students watch and listen to a film version of the entire speech. Students can write an essay supporting this statement: *Dr. King's speech is an excellent example of how to write and deliver an inspirational and motivational speech.* Students should include parts of the speech to make their points.

Model Lesson and Activity *(cont.)*

Film and Sound Recordings Model Lesson for Grades 6–12 *(cont.)*

Name_____

Using a Recording of King's "I Have a Dream" Speech

Directions: Stop the recording at the following five specific moments and discuss those sections and the meaning of the message so far.

1. Stop after the fifth paragraph that ends with "a check that will give us upon demand the riches of freedom and the security of justice." Why is the bank and check analogy so effective? How many different terms and examples does he use to strengthen the banking metaphor? Why is King pleased to be speaking at the Lincoln Memorial? Why is the analogy of the island and ocean a good choice?

2. Stop the tape after listening to the sixth and seventh paragraphs. What is the point of these two paragraphs? How does he make his case for urgency? What comparisons does he make?

3. Stop the tape after listening to the end of the statement, "We cannot turn back." What is he trying to accomplish in this section? What does he mean by "conduct our struggle on the high plane of dignity and discipline"?

4. Stop the tape after, "knowing that somehow this situation can and will be changed." What states does he target in his speech? What problems does he use to illustrate their lack of freedom?

5. Go to the end of the taped speech for the full impact of the "dream" part of the speech. How does King weave in different images of brotherhood into his dream? How does he weave in a quote from the Declaration of Independence, the Bible, a patriotic song, and a Negro spiritual to add emphasis to his dream theme?

6. What parts of his speech indicate that Dr. King is a minister? How does Dr. King's experience as a minister help him deliver such a powerful oration?

Notes

Designing Document-Based Assessments

Constructed-Response Questions

Students obviously need practice answering constructed-response questions (CRQs) and document-based essay questions (DBQs). This short overview discusses these two assessments and how teachers can design their own versions for student practice.

The purpose of constructed-response questions is to test the students' knowledge of history and the world around them. A CRQ begins with some type of map, picture, graph, chart, diagram, or other visual, and it requires students to analyze the information it contains. Each CRQ has a series of questions that must be answered.

1. The first question should be literal. It will require careful reading or studying of the document, but the answer can be found in the document. Some samples of this type of question are: Who created the document? When was it created? Who was supposed to read, see, or hear it?

2. The second question should ask for an analysis of the document. It may ask for a comparison between parts of the document or it may require a "guess," or inference about the meaning of the document. Some samples of this type of question are: Why was it created? What purpose(s) was it intended to serve? What does it tell us about the people living in that time period?

3. The final question should require using information from the document and the students' knowledge of social studies to determine the answer. It may ask students to make a prediction or to explain the significance or circumstances surrounding the document. Some samples of this type of question are: How does information provided by the document combine with other information? Does it relate to a topic today?

4. Design a CRQ scoring guide that defines the points allowed for each question. If the question has one clear, correct answer, one point is awarded. If there is a possibility of a partially correct answer, the question will have a score of two. The following are the suggested answers for the sample CRQ on page 165.

---

1. Who signed this Amnesty Oath, so that he would be pardoned and not punished for any of his actions during the Civil War?

   Score of 1—Correctly identifies Robert E. Lee.

   Score of 0—Incorrectly identifies Robert E. Lee or no response is given.

2. Explain in your own words two things the person signing promised to do.

   Score of 2—Correctly uses own words when identifying the two promises made: supporting the Constitution and abiding by laws made during rebellion, including the freedom of slaves.

   Score of 1—Only identifies one promise made in the oath.

   Score of 0—Fails to identify any promise made in the oath or no response is given.

3. What is one reason the Union might have wanted Confederate officers to sign this oath?

   Score of 1—Responds with answers such as: the Union hopes to prevent a rebellion again; the oath is used to gain support for the Union; or the oath helps to bring the country together.

   Score of 0—Fails to respond or responds very poorly.

Constructed-Response Questions *(cont.)*

Example of a Constructed-Response Question

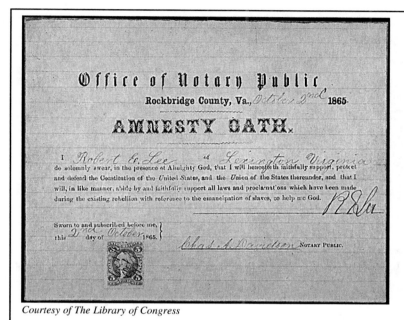

Courtesy of The Library of Congress

Text of the Amnesty Oath

I Robert E. Lee of Lexington, Virginia do solemnly swear, in the presence of Almighty God, that I will henceforth faithfully support, protect and defend the Constitution of the United States, and the Union of the States thereunder, and that I will, in like manner, abide by and faithfully support all laws and proclamations which have been made during the existing rebellion with reference to the emancipation of slaves, so help me God.

—R E. Lee

Sworn to and subscribed before me, this 2nd day of October 1865.

—Chas. A. Davidson Notary Public

Directions: Read the text of the Amnesty Oath above to answer the questions.

1. Who signed this Amnesty Oath, so that he would be pardoned and not punished for any of his actions during the Civil War?

   _____

2. Explain in your own words two things the person signing promised to do.

   _____

   _____

   _____

3. What is one reason the Union might have wanted Confederate officers to sign this oath?

   _____

   _____

   _____

How to Design a Document-Based Question

The document-based question (or DBQ) represents a real-world or authentic assessment. There are two parts to a DBQ. In the first part, students read and analyze passages, charts, graphs, cartoons, and other visuals. They are asked to respond to short-answer scaffold questions based on the individual primary sources.

The second part has a specific task that must be addressed in an essay. In the DBQ task, each student must draw on the material from the documents and from his or her own knowledge base to prepare an essay that demonstrates skills in comprehension, evaluation, and synthesis. Depending on the material, students may be asked to make comparisons and analogies, to apply knowledge to the given data, to take positions on issues or problems and support their conclusions, to explore multiple perspectives on an event or issue, or to apply historical analysis.

The DBQ is usually scored on a four-point scale using a scoring guide provided on the test so that students know what is expected. As you write DBQs, keep the following in mind.

1. Even though the DBQ task is the second part, you need to address the task in your planning to set the stage for your construction of the DBQ. Decide on a DBQ task for your students to complete. The task states the question and instructs the student to write the essay. The task presents a specific question or two that needs to be addressed in the essay, based on information found in the primary sources and from student knowledge.

2. Select a related series of primary sources. The primary sources should be chosen to illustrate different points of view and interactions related to the main DBQ task.

3. Write several short-answer questions for each primary source for the first part of the test.

4. Write a paragraph to provide a general historical context, framework, or overview for the question. It is intended to set the stage and help the students focus on the topic.

5. For the task, state the question and instruct the students to write their essays. The task presents a specific question or two that needs to be addressed in well-constructed essays containing supporting details.

6. Create a scoring guide that explains how the essay responses will be graded. By paying close attention to this scoring guide, students can discover what they need to do to receive the maximum number of points for their essays.

How to Design a Document-Based Question *(cont.)*

Examples of DBQ Tasks

Part 1 of a DBQ contains a series of primary sources: photograph, map, document, letter, poster, political cartoon, etc. Students can answer short questions about each. Choose documents that will relate to and support the upcoming task.

Part 2 of the DBQ is the task. Here are some examples of tasks to give you an idea of what types of questions are used.

DBQ Task

Basing your essay on the documents from Part 1 and on information you have learned from studying this unit, prepare a detailed response to the following prompt:

Describe three protests, documents, or events that contributed to the beginning of the American Revolution. Explain the role each one had.

DBQ Task

Basing your essay on the documents from Part 1 and on information you have learned from studying this unit, prepare a detailed response to the following prompt:

What are at least three of the conflicts faced while creating the Constitution of the United States? Explain how each conflict was resolved.

DBQ Task

Using the documents, the answers to the questions in Part 1, and your knowledge of American history in the 1800s, complete the following essay task:

Write a well-organized essay describing how Americans limited the freedom of both the American Indians and blacks in the 1800s. Compare the hardships of both groups.

How to Design a Document-Based Question *(cont.)*

Sample Document-Based Assessment Scoring Guide

The following scoring guide is a basic scoring guide that can be altered to match the details of any DBQ task essay.

Score of 4

- Addresses all key issues of the assigned task. Demonstrates understanding of the key major and minor issues by accurate analysis of at least three documents presented.
- Includes information from the documents in the body of the essay.
- Fully develops ideas about key issues using supporting evidence such as examples and details.
- Draws on relevant outside information.
- Consistently uses facts, examples, and details to support and develop the theme or thesis.
- Exhibits a logical and clear plan of organization in development of the essay.
- Expresses ideas clearly, including an introduction that is more than a restatement of the Task or Historical Context provided and an effective, persuasive conclusion that summarizes the theme or thesis.

Score of 3

- Addresses most of the key issues of the assigned task or addresses all key issues in a limited way. Provides accurate analysis of some of the documents presented.
- Includes some information from the documents in the body of the essay.
- Develops ideas satisfactorily with adequate supporting evidence.
- Includes limited relevant outside information.
- Utilizes some facts, examples, and details, but the discussion is more descriptive than analytical.
- Demonstrates a general plan of organization.
- Includes an introduction that is more than a restatement of the Task or Historical Context provided and concludes with a summation of the theme or thesis. Ideas are generally expressed clearly.

Score of 2

- Attempts to address some or all of the key issues. Uses some of the documents in a limited way.
- Uses some information from the documents in the body of the essay.
- Includes limited or no relevant outside information.
- Demonstrates weakness in development of ideas with little supporting evidence.
- Attempts to organize an answer, but is weak and lacks focus or is off task.
- Theme or thesis is not effectively introduced and there is no clear summary or conclusion.
- Attempts to express ideas clearly.

Score of 1

- Demonstrates limited understanding of the task.
- Presents no relevant outside information.
- Fails to use documents or refers only vaguely to them.
- Theme or thesis is not clearly stated or is not supported.
- Essay is poorly organized, lacks focus. Presents no clear introduction or conclusion.
- Ideas are not presented clearly.

Score of 0

- Fails to answer the question or response is totally unrelated to the topic.
- Does not use documents to support ideas.
- Uses information which is not relevant, lacks relevant details or examples.
- Lacks a plan of organization, fails to introduce or summarize a theme or thesis.
- Is incoherent; i.e., words are legible but syntax is so garbled that no sense can be made of the response.
- Is illegible or so many words cannot be read that no sense can be made of the response.

Appendix

Resources

Choosing Primary Sources for Your Classroom

Primary sources are available from many sources. Some sources are listed throughout the book and others are include here for your reference. Often the problem is not finding sources, but selecting the best sources from the many that you find from museums, archives, and the Internet. Here are a few tips to consider when selecting primary sources for your classroom.

Accessibility—Are the sources easily accessible? How will I present the source—printed copy or online? Avoid sending students on Internet searches for primary sources unless you have first attempted to find them yourself. Classroom time is too valuable to send students looking for sources that may not exist or are extremely tricky to find.

Complements Current Curriculum—Do these sources meet or enhance the current curriculum? How will I use the sources to demonstrate the main ideas of the lessons? Would this primary source give new insight into the topic we are studying? How can I assess the students' work with this source?

Length and Time Factors—Is this source the correct length to cover in the amount of time that I have? Could I use an excerpt of this source instead of the whole document? What background do I need to help students understand the excerpt?

Student Interest and Reading Level—Will my students find this source interesting or fascinating? Will they gain knowledge and skills by using this source? Is this source too easy, too difficult, or is it appropriate for my grade level? Will students need extra instruction to understand the vocabulary? Can they comprehend the document or just "read" the words?

Bias or Point of View—What is the point of view or bias of the author? How will that affect its use? How will I help students understand the bias of the creator of the source? Should I offer several sources with different points of view? Have I provided a good balance among different points of view?

Different Types of Sources—Did I include different types of sources—photographs, prints, published documents, unpublished documents, maps, and cartoons when appropriate?

Student Projects—How can my students use the primary sources in their reports, displays and electronic presentations? How can I help students determine which primary sources will best demonstrate the theme or objective of their projects?

Copyright Issues—If my students are preparing a website, what copyright issues are involved with this primary source? Using the source in a multimedia presentation in a classroom is acceptable because it is a one-time use and not published. However the Web is considered a publishing avenue and has stricter rules.

Resources *(cont.)*

Resource List

- **ABYZ News Links**—Newspapers and other news sources from around the world
  http://www.abyznewslinks.com/

- **American Rhetoric**—Famous speeches both as recordings and as written transcripts
  http://www.americanrhetoric.com/

- **The Avalon Project at Yale Law School**—History and political documents
  http://www.yale.edu/lawweb/avalon/avalon.htm

- **Center for Oral History at the University of Hawaii**—Recollections of Hawaii's people
  http://www.oralhistory.hawaii.edu/

- **CIA World Factbook**—Maps and statistics about countries around the world
  http://www.cia.gov/cia/publications/factbook/

- **Colonial Williamsburg—http://www.history.org/**
  - African American Experience—http://www.history.org/Almanack/life/Af_Amer/aalife.cfm
  - Colonial Williamsburg Multimedia Pages—http://www.history.org/media/index.cfm
  - Politics in Colonial America—http://www.history.org/Almanack/life/politics/polhdr.cfm

- **Eyewitness History.com**—Eyewitness accounts of historical events
  http://www.eyewitnesstohistory.com/

- **Hanover Historical Texts Project**—Primary sources dating from ancient to modern times.
  http://history.hanover.edu/project.html

- **History Place—Sounds of Presidents**—Presidential speeches and announcements
  http://www.historyplace.com/specials/sounds-prez/

- **Internet History Sourcebooks Project**—Public domain historical texts
  http://www.fordham.edu/halsall/

- **The Library of Congress—http://www.loc.gov**
  - American Memory—http://memory.loc.gov/ammem/
  - Global Gateway—http://international.loc.gov/intldl/intldlhome.html
  - America's Library—http://www.americaslibrary.gov
  - Thomas (legislative updates)—http://thomas.loc.gov/
  - Learning Page for Teachers—http://memory.loc.gov/learn1
  - American Folklife Center—http://www.loc.gov/folklife/
  - Veterans History Project—http://www.loc.gov/vets/

Resources *(cont.)*

Resource List *(cont.)*

- **The National Archives and Records Administration—http://www.archives.gov/**
  - Archival Research Catalog—http://www.archives.gov/research_room/arc/index.html
  - Digital Classroom—http://www.archives.gov/digital_classroom/index.html
  - History in the Raw—http://www.archives.gov/digital_classroom/history_in_the_raw.html
  - Presidential Libraries and Museums—http://www.archives.gov/presidential_libraries/index.html

    These libraries are located in presidential hometowns or birth sites: Herbert Hoover (Iowa); Franklin D. Roosevelt (New York); Harry S. Truman (Missouri); Dwight D. Eisenhower (Kansas); John F. Kennedy (Massachusetts); Lyndon B. Johnson (Texas); Gerald Ford (Michigan); James Carter (Arkansas); Ronald Reagan (California); George Bush (Texas); and William Clinton (Arkansas). The Nixon Library (California) is privately operated by a foundation. The Nixon papers (currently housed in the National Archives) are in the process of being transferred to the Nixon Library. At that time the Nixon Library will become part of the National Archives.

- **National History Day**—Main site for people interested in this yearly history competition
  http://www.nationalhistoryday.org/

- **New York Public Library**—Collections of digitized primary sources
  http://www.nypl.org/digital/

- **Newseum**—Interactive news museum
  http://www.newseum.org/

- **Old Time Radio—Radio Days: A Soundbite History**—Old radio shows and news
  http://www.otr.com

- **Our Documents**—100 milestone documents in American history
  http://www.ourdocuments.gov/

- **Political Cartoons and Cartoonists**—Digital copies of political cartoons throughout history
  http://www.boondocksnet.com/gallery/pc_intro.html

- **Smithsonian Institution—http://www.si.edu/**
  - National Museum of the American Indian—http://www.nmai.si.edu/
  - America on the Move—http://americanhistory.si.edu/onthemove/
  - The American Presidency—http://americanhistory.si.edu/presidency/

- **Sounds of History**—Over 300 sound recordings.
  http://www.sinberg.com/~history/

- **Teacher Created Materials**—Exploring History through Primary Sources kits
  http://www.teachercreatedmaterials.com/socialStudies

Credits

Image Credits

The Teacher Resource CD has copies of the images provided throughout this book. Having the digital copies will simplify completing the activities suggested in the book. All files have been saved as JPEG files so that they can be used in a variety of software programs.

Page	Figure	Filename	Title of primary source	Where original is located
4, 138	1.1, 8.1	lincoln.jpg	Contents of Abraham Lincoln's Pockets	The Library of Congress, Rare Books and Special Collections Division
4	1.2	citizen.jpg	*The Daily Citizen*—Vicksburg, Mississippi	The Library of Congress, Rare Book and Special Collections Division
5	1.3a	spurs.jpg	Silver-plated spurs	The Library of Congress, Buckaroos in Paradise: Ranching Culture in Northern Nevada, 1945–1982 (NV9-WS22-4)
5	1.3b	chisel.jpg	Old chisel	The Library of Congress, Buckaroos in Paradise: Ranching Culture in Northern Nevada, 1945–1982 (NV9-WS16-7)
5	1.4	bonds.jpg	Stamp 'em out: Buy U.S. Stamps and bonds	The Library of Congress, Prints and Photographs Division (LC-USZC2-1142)
6	1.5	letter1.jpg	Letter from Roosevelt to his son (2 pages)	The Library of Congress, Words and Deeds, Manuscript Division
6	1.6a	charley.jpg	Charley Williams and his granddaughter	The Library of Congress, Manuscript Division
6	1.6b	murphy.jpg	Fieldworker interview Anne Murphy	The Library of Congress, American Folklife Center (AFC 1995/028: WIP-MC-C054-07)
7	1.7a	baptism.jpg	Baptism near Mineola, Texas, 1935	The Library of Congress, Prints and Photographs Division
7	1.7b	imgrant1.jpg	Eastern European immigrant family	Courtesy of the Coan family
8, 127	1.8, 7.15	smith.jpg	John Smith's map of Virginia	Historical Documents Co.
8	1.9	shocked.jpg	*Harper's Weekly*—Shocked at Corruption	The Library of Congress, Prints and Photographs Division (LC-USZ62-119285)
9	1.10	brigade1.jpg	The Black Brigade: Plantation Song & Dance	The Library of Congress, Rare Books and Special Collections Division
9	1.10	brigade2.jpg	The Black Brigade: Plantation Song & Dance	The Library of Congress, Rare Books and Special Collections Division
11	1.11	seal.jpg	First Seal of Plymouth	Recreated by Teacher Created Materials
12	1.12	labor.jpg	Child laborers in Macon, Georgia	The National Archives, Still Picture Records (ARC 523148; Record Group 102)
13	1.13a	street1.jpg	Virginia intersection in 1935	Courtesy of Kathryn Kiley
13	1.13b	street2.jpg	Virginia intersection today	Courtesy of Emily R. Smith
14	1.14	notebook.jpg	Walt Whitman's hospital notebook	The Library of Congress, Manuscript Division, Walt Whitman Collection
15, 38	1.15, 2.27	bison.jpg	Bison hide yard in 1878	The National Archives, Still Picture Records (ARC 520093; Record Group 79)
16	1.16	letter2.jpg	Truman's letter to his girlfriend (8 pages)	The National Archives, Truman Presidential Museum and Library
20	2.1	flagstaf.jpg	Flagstaff, Arizona	The National Archives, Still Picture Records (ARC 516371; Record Group 48)
20	2.2	imgrant2.jpg	Mediterranean immigrants	Courtesy of the Burton family
22	2.3	n/a	American Indian family	Denver Public Library, Western History Collection, Charles Nast, X-30762
24	2.4	declare.jpg	Drafting the Declaration of Independence	The National Archives, Still Picture Records (ARC 513332; Record Group 30)
25	2.5	columbus.jpg	Columbus with the king and queen	The Library of Congress, Prints and Photographs Division (LC-USZC2-1589)
26	2.6	johnjay.jpg	Portrait of John Jay	The Library of Congress, Prints and Photographs Division (LC-D416-9856)
26	2.7	william.jpg	William the Conqueror	The Library of Congress, Prints & Photographs Division (LC-USZ62-120673)
27	2.8a	angel.jpg	Angel Island	The Library of Congress, Historic American Buildings (HABS, CAL, 21-ANGEL)
27	2.8b	roundup.jpg	Roundup at the Ranch	The National Archives, Still Picture Records (ARC 533791; Record Group 165)

Credits *(cont.)*

Image Credits *(cont.)*

Page	Figure	Filename	Title of primary source	Where original is located
27	2.8c	berlin.jpg	Building the Berlin Wall	Courtesy of Betsy Morris
27	2.8d	duomo.jpg	Florence *Duomo*	Courtesy of Rachelle Cracchiolo
27	2.8e	lee.jpg	General Robert E. Lee	The National Archives, Still Picture Records (ARC 525769; Record Group 111)
28	2.9	dust.jpg	Kansas dust storm	The National Archives, Franklin D. Roosevelt Library
28	2.10	bridge.jpg	St. Louis Eads Bridge	The Library of Congress, Prints and Photographs Division (LC-USZC4-4899)
29	2.11	iwojima.jpg	Flag raising on Iwo Jima	The National Archives, Still Picture Records (ARC 520748; Record Group 80)
29	2.12	unemploy.jpg	Unemployment in America	The National Archives, Franklin D. Roosevelt Library
30	2.13	mulberry.jpg	Mulberry Street in New York City	The Library of Congress, Prints and Photographs Division (LC-D401-12683)
30	2.14	railroad.jpg	Meeting of the Transcontinental Railroad	The National Archives
31	2.15	pompeii.jpg	Amphitheater in Pompeii	Courtesy of the Burton Family
31	2.16	charlstn.jpg	Ruins of Charleston	The National Archives, Still Picture Records (ARC 528874, Record Group 111)
31	2.17	indphall.jpg	Interior of Independence Hall	The Library of Congress, Historic American Buildings Survey (HABS,PA,51-PHILA,6-56)
32	2.18	migrant.jpg	Migrant Mother	The National Archives, Franklin D. Roosevelt Library
32	2.19	fireside.jpg	Fireside Chat	The National Archives, Franklin D. Roosevelt Library
32	2.20	drummer.jpg	Drummer boy from the Civil War	The National Archives, Still Picture Records (ARC 533233, Record Group 165)
33	2.21	kingtut.jpg	King Tutankhamen's mask	Courtesy of the Burton Family
33	2.22	totem.jpg	Tlingit totem pole	The Woods Publishing Group
33	2.23	apple.jpg	Early Apple computer	Courtesy of Emily R. Smith
34	2.24	fedhall.jpg	Federal Hall	The Library of Congress, Prints and Photographs Division (PRES FILE)
34	2.25	russia.jpg	Russia for Justice poster	The Library of Congress, Prints and Photographs Division (LC-USZ62-5025)
35	2.26	sewing.jpg	Home sewing business	The National Archives, Still Picture Records (Record Group 102)
41	2.28	cable.jpg	Eighth Wonder of the World	The Library of Congress, Prints and Photographs Division (LC-USZC4-2388)
47	3.1	compact.jpg	Mayflower Compact	Historical Documents Co.
48	3.2	tavern.jpg	Rules of this tavern sign	Historical Documents Co.
48	3.3	auction.jpg	Slave auction sign	Recreated by The Woods Publishing Group
49	3.4	naacp.jpg	NAACP membership drive poster	Recreated by The Woods Publishing Group
49	3.5	wecando.jpg	We Can Do It!	The National Archives (Record Group 179)
49	3.6	powmia.jpg	POW-MIA symbol	Recreated by The Woods Publishing Group
50	3.7	james.jpg	Wanted poster for the James brothers	Historical Documents Co.
50	3.8	boycott.jpg	German boycott poster	Recreated by Teacher Created Materials
51	3.9	ration.jpg	War ration book	Courtesy of the Smith and Mulhall families
51	3.10	border.jpg	Application for a border permit card	Immigration and Naturalization Service
58	3.11	notice.jpg	German advertisement from 1915	*The New York Times*
59	3.12	election.jpg	Lincoln election poster from 1860	The National Archives
76	4.1	wright.jpg	Wright Brothers telegram	The Library of Congress, Manuscript Division (LC-MSS-46706-5)

Credits *(cont.)*

Image Credits *(cont.)*

Page	Figure	Filename	Title of primary source	Where original is located
77	4.2	letter3.jpg	Letter to the president (2 pages)	The National Archives, John F. Kennedy Library (ARC #193938; Collection: JFK-RFK)
78	4.3	myself.jpg	Page from first draft of "Song of Myself"	The Library of Congress, Notebook LC #80
78	4.4	sketch.jpg	Alexander Graham Bell's telephone sketch	The Library of Congress, Manuscript Division
87	4.5	dday.jpg	"In Case of Failure Message"	The National Archives, Dwight D. Eisenhower Library
98	6.1	joindie.jpg	"Join, or Die" cartoon	Recreated by The Woods Publishing Company
99	6.2	pillars.jpg	"The Federal Pillars" cartoon	The Library of Congress, Prints and Photographs Division (LC-USZ62-45589)
99	6.3	slaves.jpg	"Fugitive Slave Act" cartoon	The Library of Congress, Prints and Photographs Division (LC-USZC4-4660)
100	6.4	footrace.jpg	"Presidential Footrace" cartoon	The Library of Congress, Prints and Photographs Division (LC-USZ62-14834)
101	6.5	nast1.jpg	"Stone Walls Do Not a Prison Make" cartoon	The Library of Congress, Prints and Photographs Division (LC-USZ6-951)
101	6.6	nast2.jpg	"Tweed-le-dee and Tilden-dum" cartoon	The Library of Congress, Prints and Photographs Division (LC-USZ62-117137)
102	6.7	walk.jpg	"I Think I'll Walk" cartoon	The Library of Congress, Prints and Photographs Division (LC-USZ62-125623)
102	6.8	togo.jpg	"To Go or Not to Go" cartoon	The National Archives, Center for Legislative Archives (ARC 306086, Record Group 46)
103	6.9	grtrace.jpg	"The Great Race for the Western Stakes" cartoon	The Library of Congress, Prints and Photographs Division (LC-USZC2-2531)
104	6.10	bluff.jpg	"Play Bluff" cartoon	Recreated by The Woods Publishing Group
106	6.11	feud.jpg	Neighborhood feud cartoon	The National Archives, Center for Legislative Archives (ARC 306137, Record Group 46)
106	6.12	chore.jpg	"A Real Chore" cartoon	The National Archives
107	6.13	truman.jpg	Truman comic book	The National Archives, Truman Presidential Museum and Library
108	6.14	n/a	"Shucks! Is That All?" cartoon strip	Tribune Media Services, Inc.
108	6.15	n/a	"Down, but Not Out" cartoon strip	Tribune Media Services, Inc.
110	6.16	voting.jpg	"Election Day!" cartoon	The Library of Congress, Prints and Photographs Division (LC-USZ62-51821)
112	6.17	carnegie.jpg	"The Macmillion" cartoon	The Library of Congress, Prints and Photographs Division
114	6.18	missrvr.jpg	"Life on the Mississippi" cartoon	The National Archives, Center for Legislative Archives (ARC 306097, Record Group 46)
119	7.1	calif.jpg	Old map of California	Historical Documents Co.
119	7.2	missouri.jpg	Bird's-eye view of Kansas City, Missouri	The Library of Congress, Geography and Map Division (G4164.K2A3 1869 .R8)
120	7.3	iraq.jpg	Archaeological map of Iraq	The Library of Congress, Geography and Map Division (G7611.E15 1967 .I7)
120	7.4	iowa.jpg	Railroad map of Iowa	The Library of Congress, Geography and Map Division (G4151.P3 1881 .I6 RR 219)
121	7.5	ciamap.jpg	CIA map of the Indian Ocean	The Library of Congress, Geography and Map Division (G9180 1986.U5)
121	7.6	dachau.jpg	Map of Dachau	Recreated by Teacher Created Materials
122	7.7	n/a	Ancient clay tablet	The Semitic Museum, Harvard University
123	7.8	ptolemy.jpg	Map by Claudius Ptolemy	The Library of Congress, Geography and Map Division
124	7.9	mercator.jpg	Mercator projection map	Teacher Created Materials
125	7.10	waldsmlr.jpg	1507 world map by Martin Waldseemüller	The Library of Congress, Geography and Map Division (G3200 1507 .W3)
125 132	7.11 7.21	speed.jpg	1651 world map by John Speed	Historical Documents Co.
126	7.12	mollmap.jpg	1719 world map by Hermon Moll	The Library of Congress, Geography and Map Division (G3200 1719.M6 TIL Vault)
126	7.13	careymap.jpg	1795 world map by Mathew Carey	The Library of Congress, Geography and Map Division (G3200 1795.C3 TIL Vault)

Credits (cont.)

Image Credits (cont.)

Page	Figure	Filename	Title of primary source	Where original is located
127	7.14	whitemap.jpg	John White's map of Virginia	The Library of Congress, Geography and Map Division (G3880 1590.W4)
128	7.16	survey.jpg	Washington's survey map	The Library of Congress, Geography and Map Division (G3820 1754. W3 1927)
128	7.17	bauman.jpg	Sebastian Bauman's map for General Washington	The Library of Congress, Geography and Map Division (G3884.Y6S3 1782 .B3 Vault)
129	7.18	1783map.jpg	1783 United States map	The Library of Congress, Geography and Map Division (G3700 1783.W3 Vault)
129	7.19	oklahoma.jpg	Oklahoma Territory map	The Library of Congress, Map and Geography Division (G402.1.E1 1892.M2 TIL Vault)
130	7.20	railway.jpg	Union Pacific Railway map	The Library of Congress, Geography and Map Division (G3701.P3 1883 .R36 RR 595)
138	8.2	gauge.jpg	Gauge	National Frontier Trails Museum
139	8.3a	bonnet.jpg	Bonnet	National Frontier Trails Museum
139	8.3b	pwdrhorn.jpg	Powder horn	National Frontier Trails Museum
139	8.3c	coffee.jpg	Coffee mill	National Frontier Trails Museum
139	8.3d	packsdle.jpg	Packsaddle	National Frontier Trails Museum
140	8.4	stencil.jpg	Waggoner Gates Milling Co. iron stencil	National Frontier Trails Museum
140	8.5	marker.jpg	Marking gauge	National Frontier Trails Museum
143	8.6	hileman1.jpg	Keil Hileman's classroom	Courtesy of Keil Hileman
143	8.7	hileman2.jpg	Keil Hileman's classroom	Courtesy of Keil Hileman
144	8.8	hileman3.jpg	Keil Hileman's classroom	Courtesy of Keil Hileman
151	9.1	phono1.jpg	Phonograph advertisement	The Library of Congress, American Memory
152	9.2	phono2.jpg	The Edison concert phonograph	The Library of Congress, Prints and Photographs Division (LC-USZC2-5742)
153	9.3	banner.jpg	"The Star Spangled Banner" sheet music	The Library of Congress, Manuscript Division
165	n/a	oath.jpg	General Robert E. Lee's amnesty oath	The Library of Congress

Additional Credits

The ideas in this book are from the author's own teaching experiences, her imagination, extensive research on using primary sources, her coordination of Project WhistleStop (a United States Challenge Grant partnership with four school districts), as well as her work with the University of Missouri at Columbia and the Truman Presidential Museum and Library.

Since the author has attended workshops provided by the National Archives and Records Administration, it is natural that some concepts in this book are based on the work done over the years by the Education Staff at the National Archives. Their pioneer efforts in encouraging teachers to use primary sources in the classroom must be recognized and appreciated by all who provide training of teachers in the use of primary sources.

Thank you to Leni Donlan for the help she provided in the early stages of writing this book. Her planning and ideas for the book were invaluable in the overall direction that the book took.

The author wishes to thank Keil Hileman for generously sharing his teaching strategies for incorporating artifacts into classroom activities. These strategies and the pictures of his classroom greatly enhanced the chapter on artifacts.